Dedication

We dedicate this book to all those who have given us the strength to fulfill our dreams of writing and our parents, whose blessings have been a driving force in achieving our dreams.

EMPOWER TO TRANSFORM

Transform to Empower

NIRAJA BANDI
and
ARGHYA CHAKRABORTY

XpressPublishing

An imprint of Notion Press

No.8, 3rd Cross St, CIT Colony,
Mylapore, Chennai,
Tamil Nadu - 600004

First Published by Notion Press 2021
Copyright © Niranja Bandi and Arghya Chakraborty 2021
All Rights Reserved.

ISBN 978-1-63781-856-5

Contents

Contents

Contents

Contents

Author's Note

"Empower to Transform" is an in-depth analysis of gender inequality and some of the concepts that revolve around it. This aspect that has received a lot of attention from researchers still remains a mystery to most people. Due to the lack of understanding on the matter, most women find themselves unable to pull through from the chains that oppress and prevent them from achieving success.

This analysis starts by exploring the effects and dangers of atrocities on women. It then digs deeper to matters related to equality at home and work, diversity and inclusion, women in leadership, role of men in women empowerment and empower to transform.

Other than introducing the society to the merits of women empowerment, this is a guide that will motivate and inspire women of all ages, races and ethnicities to revolt against the social injustice that they face.

It's not your ordinary self-help book as it dives into the core issues that need to be addressed when it comes to empowering women. That aside, this book also touches on some of the most sensitive topics such as diversity and inclusion which not only affect women but also people of different races.

Full of well-researched and discussed topics, this is a book that will change your perspective towards gender equality. Written for both women and men, "Empower to Transform" leaves you with a lot of valuable information long after you have turned the final page.

Preface

Growing up, we witnessed first-hand how society treated women unfairly. At home, most mothers were tasked only with domestic duties, and family decisions were always decided by men. As we furthered our studies at the university, we couldn't help but notice the senior positions such as chancellors, dean of studies, and head of departments were always occupied by men. Another observation that we made was that programs or courses that were perceived as 'complex' had more male professors than their female counterparts.

These observations got us thinking, why is the society set up that way? And as our young minds tried to make sense of all these things, we graduated and joined the job market. After years of being in the financial services industry, we couldn't help but ponder on how greatly gender inequality has infiltrated our organizations and society in general.

Most of the companies that we have interacted with in the past don't meet the diversity and inclusion requirements. This is despite these companies operating and serving in a diverse country. Looking at the leadership, there is zero reflection of diversity.

Because we have always had a passion for mentoring team members, we decided to come up with the book Empower to Transform. Our objectives are to educate, inform, and inspire all women out there that they should know their rights, raise their voice, and fight for the atrocities that have and continue to be committed to them.

We chose this topic because women are not only the most beautiful and intelligent creatures on earth. These beings ensure the survival of the human race. They are kind, passionate, loving, and deserve to be treated better. The topic "Empower to Transform" captures all there is about gender inequality and fair treatment. It teaches the society, the benefits of empowering women and also introduces us to some of the ways we can make this happen. It challenges men to take part in this process and ensure their counterparts are uplifted emotionally, spiritually, and financially.

Our key motivation behind writing "Empower to Transform" was our vision of a society where women have equal opportunities to men. At the moment, we have made a lot of achievements in health, technology, business, entertainment, and many more industries. This has happened when only a few women have been included in these efforts. Imagine how successful we would be if more women were involved in politics, governance, management, and research?

Inspired by the likes of Rosa Parks, Mother Teresa, Oprah Winfrey, Amelia Earhart, and other iconic women, we believe that our book will challenge most women to speak up, be more confident and make the most out of their lives.

As mentioned above, "Empower to Transform" dives into some of the atrocities committed on women. Acts such as gender-based violence, rape, and infanticide slow down the progress being made by female rights activists and women in general. The theme of this book revolves around empowerment and transformation. The discussions that you will read aim at empowering women so that they can transform into better versions of themselves and transform the society we live in.

Living in a modern era has shown us that women are equally as gifted and if given the chance, they can perform better even than men. Other than highlighting the unfair treatment of females, this book encourages women to know their rights, be ambitious, and not afraid of seeking opportunities. It also challenges the society to do away with stereotypes and false perceptions that are taking us back instead of driving the world forward.

The purpose of this book is mainly to create awareness of women's empowerment. From historical monuments and documentaries, women have always been undermined and belittled in the society. In the past, a woman's place was in the kitchen and to bear children. To show you how serious this was, a woman who gave birth to girl children only was deemed unfit. And in some traditional cultures, girl children weren't even celebrated.

Even though things aren't as extreme as they were in the past, we still have a long way to go. Women are yet to be empowered. Ask yourself the following questions; how many female presidents do you know of? Out of all the organizations you have visited, what is the ratio of men to women? As a woman, do you feel like you are in control of your life? For men, are the women in your life empowered?

If most of your answers are no, then there is a lot you can learn from this book. Are you sick and tired of gender inequality and watching women being mistreated? As you flip the pages of this self-help book, you will understand all the concepts related to empowerment and transformation. As a result, you will gain skills and useful information that will help combat and prevent atrocities females face every day.

The journey of writing this book started on one fine evening after coming across a news story on how the Covid-19 pandemic has led to an increase of incidents in domestic violence. From the reporter's face, we could see how frustrated she felt when reading the statistics. Due to the lockdowns, most couples had to stay for extended hours in their homes, and this caused a lot of tension in most homes.

And as if that's not enough, the same women were also overburdened by domestic chores. After looking up the matter even further, we realized that the effects of the pandemic were particularly more severe to women than men. Females who had to work at home found it next to impossible to operate under distractions from kids, their husbands, and the chores they had to do. Fast forward towards the end of the pandemic, most women couldn't return to their jobs because of falling behind on many projects.

Disappointed by these occurrences, we found ourselves writing the first chapter that is based on atrocities on women. This real-life situation inspired us to write "Empower to Transform" and encourage women out there to raise their voices. With so many wrongs being done unto women, it was our moral duty to speak on them and condemn all these vices. Within the book, you will realize that we are very particular when it comes to making amendments on diversity and inclusion.

The book "Empower to Transform" has also gone the extra mile to discuss issues related to race and age gaps in the work environment. We can't talk about diversity and empowerment without addressing the issues of racism. We live in a world full of people from different races. The 21st century has made it possible for anyone to live anywhere and still enjoy their freedoms and rights.

However, just because you are in a foreign land, you shouldn't have a limit on the things you can or can't do. This book looks at some of the elements that affect minorities based on their gender or race. Stereotypes that have led us to follow these practices are highlighted and discouraged.

We can't deny that during both the writing and research process, we have learned and gained a lot. We have come to understand that toxic masculinity or femininity won't solve the gender inequality vice that has lingered on for centuries. It has also come to our attention that both men and women need to contribute to empowering women. Other lessons learned from writing this book include; the importance of being patient and understanding, the power of forgiveness, and the willingness to move forward despite any challenges we may face.

Writing this book was quite interesting to us. And we have to say that we really enjoyed discovering new ideas related to empowering women to transform. The research process was however quite extensive and because our objective was to write a detailed analysis of women empowerment, we had to spend a lot of time digging out information. The internet proved exceptionally useful as it led us to many resources. Most of the time we found ourselves overwriting because of how much there is to say about empowering women.

As described above, the research process was quite exciting. My colleague and I had to read different books related to women empowerment and gender inequality so that we could find the right theme for this book. After choosing a theme, we came up with a plot for the book and divided these topics into chapters. Most of the research was from non-governmental resources such as the United Nations. We also referred to scholarly articles from other experts in the field.

We would like to acknowledge our colleagues for their significant participation in this book. These brilliant minds helped us come up with the original idea for this book. During the writing process, they encouraged us plenty of times and assisted with resources where we got the most information from.

"Empower to Transform" is a book written for everyone. It can be used for both educational and informational purposes. And to get the most out of it, we recommend following the chapters in the order provided.

For those whom we share a passion for women empowerment and transformation, allow us to introduce you to what we have discovered. After centuries of women being treated unfairly, we finally believe there is a solution that can guarantee long term changes. The issue of empowering women has been a hot topic of debate in newsrooms, lecture halls, and even offices. But very little has been done to enhance measures that will see women being empowered.

This book has compiled several strategies that will ensure fair treatment of all women out there. Through creating awareness and sensitizing the public on adopting these policies, with time, we are going to reap the benefits of a country full of ambitious, powerful, and determined women. we long for the day when we will walk into an office full of more ladies than gents. Or a situation where nearly all success stories are in one way directed to a woman.

The solutions given in this book are realistic, and if we can all take the time to read it carefully and understand each and every concept, then the force to empower women will be unstoppable. Let us not leave this fight to women's activists or non-governmental organizations, the entire society should be involved. Because, when women are transformed, they will give back to the society without picking those who did or didn't campaign for their empowerment. Even if you are not a woman, think about your mother/guardian, sister, niece, cousin, or even a female friend. Wouldn't it be in your best interest to empower them?

As an avid reader, we recognize that there aren't as many books out there similar to this one. This is what makes this book so perfect for anyone championing for women's rights. Everything that we dug out in our research, we have shared it in this book. You can also expect to find statistics related to gender inequality, diversity, and inclusion.

Acknowledgments

In a VUCA world deluged by irrelevant information, clarity is power. From Rigveda, we know that a person becomes a scholar from knowledge, and proper application of the knowledge, helps a person transform himself/herself. The best way to transform and get addicted to the intangible weapon is to read books. From a writer's perspective, we accept that writing any book is a massive undertaking, and no author does it alone.

We want to extend our sincere thanks and heartfelt gratitude to our mentors who have guided and motivated us to put in our thoughts through writing. Authors Som Bathla and Sweta Samota, our mentors in the authorpreneur journey who inspired us to write. Their guidance at every step has been precious, without which it wasn't possible to complete this book.

Thank you, our valued readers, for having faith in us and investing your valuable time reading this book. Thanks for being part of this journey. When women are finally empowered in society, may the transformation benefit us all. To our colleagues, thanks for your support both professionally and on a personal level. Special mention to our colleagues Prof. Anupama Rawat, Praneeth Chandra, Dr. Abhishek Tripathi, Dr. Vijay Robert, and Ratna Rao, who have given their valuable suggestions throughout the writing journey. To our family, thanks for being there during the entire period.

We have learned a lot from you and used the knowledge you have passed onto us in writing this book.

We believe that a united society can never be defeated. In this fight against empowerment to transform, let's join hands and create awareness on gender inequality. Feel free to use anything that you will learn in this book to make our world a better place where women are celebrated, appreciated, and, most importantly, EMPOWERED!

If suddenly you do not exist,

if suddenly you no longer live,

I shall live on.

I do not dare,

I do not dare to write it,

if you die.

I shall live on.

For where a man has no voice,

there, my voice.

Where blacks are beaten,

I cannot be dead.

When my brothers go to prison

I shall go with them.

When victory,

not my victory,

but the great victory comes,

even though I am mute I must speak;

xxi

I shall see it come even

though I am blind.

No, forgive me.

If you no longer live,

if you, beloved, my love,

if you have died,

all the leaves will fall in my breast,

it will rain on my soul night and day,

the snow will burn my heart,

I shall walk with frost and fire and death and snow,

my feet will want to walk to where you are sleeping, but

I shall stay alive,

because above all things

you wanted me indomitable,

and, my love, because you know that I am not only a man

but all mankind.

By Pablo Neruda

CHAPTER 1

Introduction

Isn't it a pity that……?

Isn't it a pity that?

everything in this world seems to be hurled against the Woman who is at odd

Everyone there trying to even her out at par with men again on the same men's accord!

just to be at par, is that her real ordeal?

no one really cares how different is she, and what is her inner feel.

in this world nothing seems equal nor very fair

man and woman who ought to complement

why at times stand opposed and both in despair?

gender inequality runs so deep

Being a barman is easy but

being a woman not so easy indeed

everywoman is made to be so stereo typed

and made to understood that she can't think alike with the men of her tribe

she poses a question to you and to your worldly ways

why we are not at par when

nature puts us together always

Would you ever give me a benefit of doubt?

perfect I am not though, nor that stout

frail I might look, still I nurture a dream

to live in a fairer world, where

everything is up to ..up to my self esteem

don't break my bone and make me bleed

Every drop of blood I have used in my womb for you to feed

One who gives birth and creates

can never be dumb but resonates

listen to her tunes that fills up your beautiful life

treat her as your friend, be it mother daughter or your wife.

The companion of your life is struggling hard

to fill vibrant colors in a mundane lifeless picture card

Bring her the paints and build around her the walls of your love

she will fill them up with colors of your dream and pictures of more love.

Is Gender Inequality still an issue? The answer is yes. While everyone knows the integral role played by women at home, work, and in the county, there still exists discrimination based on gender. Equality in men and women is seen when both sexes can equally share power distribution as well as influence. While there have been some notable improvements in the gender gap, there still exists gender differences, especially in developing countries.

Some argue that gender equality is increasing worldwide. A study conducted by Dorius and Firebaugh, which investigated the global trends in gender inequality, analyzed education, political representation, and mortality, noted a reduction in gender inequalities among different groups. However, there's overwhelming evidence which still shows that gender inequality is still a huge problem. It is, therefore, crucial to put gender analysis measures in place.

Discrimination, apart from women, also affects men of color, poor men, gay men, etc. who continue to be discriminated against, every day, because of their race, economy, and sex. However, it is women who still are affected most by violence, poverty, as well as inequality in the workplace and at home. For instance, according to a report by the UN Women in 2015, women worldwide earn 24% less than men. The gender gap in employment is still persistent. Worse is seen in education where several factors like sexual harassment prevent girls from accessing school.

Women, like men, play an important role in the economy of a nation considering that they make up 50% of the population. Their inclusion in all facets of the economy is therefore paramount not just to promote gender equality but also to bring general economic growth. A woman's empowerment positively influences her children, family, society, and the nation at large.

The post-2015 sustainable development agenda aimed at shifting from unsustainable policies towards those that promote sustainable production and consumption while protecting the susceptible along with improving nations' and communities' resilience to climate risks and other environmental ones. These can only be achieved when there exists gender equality that ensures the protection of human rights, social justice as well as equality between genders.

UNDP acknowledges that some progress has been noted on several Millennium Development Goals (MDGs), including a decline in poverty, child mortality along with illiteracy in various dimensions like economic crises. It also notes that gender inequality has been recognized as an obstacle to many development goals. Therefore, nations that want significant development ought to adopt gender-inclusive growth strategies that invest in empowering women to participate fully in economic development.

Active participation of women is widely acknowledged, especially in agriculture. However, many women still face challenges like segmented labor markets, discriminatory laws, restrictive practices, etc. that retard their efforts. While getting rid of gender inequalities contributes to a country's growth, many countries are still dealing with this issue. Although there has been some progress made in the last 30 years, thanks to women's movements and UN world conferences, up to today, no country has fully achieved real equality between genders.

This book reviews the place of women today with the advancement of gender equality and addresses the gaps that are still present in creating an equal world. Key issues that relate to unequal relations of power that have been addressed include educational empowerment, political empowerment, economic empowerment as well as land tenure empowerment.

Conclusions drawn indicate that society is still far from achieving gender equality. Although many states, through women's movements, have put legislative and other measures to address gender inequality, women are still discriminated worldwide because of lack of capacity, resources, persistent cultural attitudes, and less commitment for legislators and other key roles.

The book is concerned mainly with the progress that's been made on gender issues across the globe, specifically if whether gender equality has been achieved or not. It also gives solutions to how nations can tackle social, political, and economic issues that obstruct gender inequality. It considers the effects that political, social, and economic shifts have on the lives of both women and men at national as well as international levels. Additionally, it also addresses how various groups are resisting and challenging inequalities and how they're attempting to correct the root causes of gender power imbalances in an attempt to answer these questions:

How does gender equality relate to sustainable development?

What influence can women have on sustainable development?

What are the strategies that can be employed to put a stop to gender inequality and promote women's empowerment?

After doing some research on women's place in society, its concluded that women are often victimized, and society is yet to accept them as key contributors to the economy. The authors felt the need to address this issue. Through research, the authors have outlined the structures that can be adopted to achieve gender equality in all sectors.

Readers will learn about good practices and innovative educational approaches that will promote gender equality. This book explores the ways to reduce threats to girl's education and strategies for dealing with gender-based violence in schools. Research on this study examines how effective life skills education is in helping boys to develop gender-equitable behavior and attributes.

Readers will also get to know the informal rules that shape attitudes and their impact on gender equality as well as women's empowerment. This book researches the causes of discriminatory and harmful norms and proposes incredible strategies of gender justice. It also identifies where and how gender norms deter girls from accessing education and exclude women from the decision-making process. It also proposes solutions for achieving gender equality in political, legal, civic, and economic structures.

This book is presenting a new paradigm for societies as well as nations to ensure equality. However, it isn't just a theoretical presentation. Readers will learn how they can participate in empowering women through ending discrimination, gender-based violence, and unequal pay gap with an ethical and successful approach.

To counter gender inequality, in the initial chapters, we investigate female infanticide, which is also known as gender-selective killing of girl babies. This is one of the many atrocities committed on women. The reader also introduces other forms of violence against women which include rape, domestic marriage, mistreatment, forced marriage etc. In this book, we list ways on how to end violence towards women.

From a woman's point of view, the following chapters titled raise your voice and know your rights are meant to help women discover their place in the society. All humans share the same rights and freedom. Once we understand our rights, it will be impossible to watch atrocities being committed on us. Once you know your rights, then you can raise your voice and defend yourself.

Gender inequality, another form of atrocity is dedicated an entire chapter. And readers can get the definition of this practice and remedy for this vice that has caused suffering to women in all corners of the world.

We have also explored equality at home and in the workplace. Gone are the days when the woman's role was only in the kitchen. The modern woman knows her strengths and isn't afraid to use them to her advantage. In a domestic relationship, a couple ought to define roles irrespective of gender. Both parents should take care of the child, and the woman shouldn't have to quit work to be a "stay at home" mom.

On the other side of things, at the workplace, who said that some positions belong to men and not women? This leads us to our next chapter on women in leadership. For decades, managerial and top positions only belonged to men. But from recent data, we have seen organizations being led by women thriving beyond everyone's expectations. Thanks to some of the unique characteristics possessed by women, they make excellent leaders, role models and mentors.

We can all agree that women deserve to be empowered. But who is to be tasked with this 'job' of empowering women? The chapter, role of men in women empowerment', discusses how men have been in power for so long and how hard it is for women to infiltrate this space. Men have a key role in empowering women. And this should start from home all the way to the workplace. A husband shouldn't be afraid of letting his wife make some of the key decisions in the house, after all, all she wants is to do right for her family.

At the workplace, the board of directors should understand that women have a role to play as well. And as a result, ensure fair recruitment and equal treatment in a work environment. This takes us to the chapter on diversity and inclusion. The world is a diverse place. We have men, women and even the LGBTQ community.

There are people of different races, ethnicity, ages and other demographics.

It is important that every organization ensures inclusivity in the workplace. And this can start by granting women fair treatment, involving them in decision making, ensuring that the leadership is diverse and making the workplace more diverse and comfortable. From all these efforts, we are guaranteed of empowering women to transform into a better version of themselves.

Through the in-depth discussions of topics, the society can learn the importance of appreciating women in their lives. Not forgetting that they make up most of the world's population, it is only fair that they are accorded the respect that they deserve. With many practices listed, the society can cultivate a set of good moral principles. Living in a world full of criticism, racism and sexism alongside other vices, we need to find a new way forward that is diverse and inclusive.

CHAPTER 2

Female Infanticide

She was a pearl,

a beautiful GIRL

trying to take shelter in this

materialistic world.

You yourself,

became so materialistic.

Your polluted mind,

dropped her down.

That drop lost her existnce,

with the lost bemoan.

- Anamika

What is Female Infanticide?

Female infanticide is an intentional killing of female children. The act is also described as femicide, gendercide, or selective killing. Birth of children by unmarried women, dowry system, and the birth of deformed children, famine, and maternal illnesses are some of the factors attributed to infanticide. It was practiced by both primitive and sophisticated cultures all over the world. The reasons behind female infanticide were cultural, and many religions condemned the act. Societies that practice the act are always gender-biased and perceive women as caregivers and homemakers, while men predominantly dictate family's economic and social stability.

Origin of Female Infanticide

Infanticide was common in areas with high population and was practiced to restrict population and poverty. Historically, infanticide was the only effective method used to curb starvation and low living standards. In India some parents were forced to kill girls to remain with the number they could comfortably take care of.

Christian missionaries made some documentation on the culture in the 19th century. They wrote a letter on their accomplishments in India and described the culture as ignorant and savage. Some scholars have questioned these conclusions on Indian cultures made during the colonial period claiming that infanticide was as common in England as it was in India.

A Subaltern studies group member: David Arnold used many contemporary resources to conclude that various infanticide methods were used.

In 1991 the Indian government launched the Girl child protection scheme. The scheme acted as a long-term financial relief for rural families to meet essential obligations like mothers' sterilization. The fund increased as the girl grew older to allow them to marry or continue with their education.

In 1992, the government started the baby cradle scheme, allowing parents to give up their children for adoption without going through the official procedures. This scheme has saved thousands of children. However, the scheme has received a lot of criticism from human rights agencies, claiming that it encourages child abandonment and reinforces the low status in which women are viewed. In the first four years of the scheme, 136 baby girls were given anonymously for adoption. In 2000, 1218, female infanticide cases were witnessed, making the scheme ineffective.

In 2011, the government of India introduced "Beti Bachao, Beti Padhao" initiative. The initiative was motivated by 2011 census results, which showed a remarkable decline in gender balance. The government intends to use the initiative to curb gender discrimination by ensuring girls' survival and education.

Indian legislation does not allow any form of female infanticide and prenatal sex selection. The legislation prohibits any advertisements on prenatal diagnosis with the intention of sex selection. However, these laws are hard to implement; therefore, it is essential to offer girls and women, empowerment in India.

Hinduism and Female Infanticide

Female infanticide was widely practiced by barbaric Vedic's who lived in India. They portrayed great hate for women and considered female children undesirable. Women were also not allowed to read the great Vedas holy book, a Hindu guide. The large dowry imposed on women made them look like economic burdens for their families and the community. Women were also not of great use during the war; thus, their numbers were reduced to maintain the Aryan war team's high effectiveness.

However, Hindu leaders condemn infanticide and claim that Hindu's preference for male children is entirely based on the fact that men are better providers than women. Men are also important when performing death and funeral rites.

Confucianism and female infanticide

Confucianism says "value the boy and disdain the female" this saying might seem old. However, it is still relevant to Chinese people, where males carry the family legacy and are referred to as the source of security and economic stability. Since china value family heritage, the desire for boys has led many families to kill or abort female children. Confucianism regards male children more superior to girls because of their roles in the family and the community.

Sikhism

Sikh leaders do not support infanticide. The Sikh religion supports gender equality; it's the most gender-neutral religion. However, the census shows that there are more male children than girls in the Sikh region. It is also surprising that even in these communities, most families prefer having male children over female. The Sikh community has emphasized male-female equality and has discouraged neonatal sex identification, female infanticide, and selective abortion.

Islam

Female infanticide was common during pre-Islamic Arabia. However, during the time of Prophet Mohammed, female infanticide was highly condemned. It was regarded as murder. Christianity and Judaism also condemned infanticide.

Female infanticide in India

Section 315 of the Indian penal code differentiates infanticide from other crimes by offering a precise definition: infanticide is killing an infant in the 0-1 age group. Infanticide was first noticed by British colonialists in 1785, during the time of company rule. According to Marvin Harris, an anthropologist, cultural and economic reasons were the main reasons for female child killings, especially among the Rajput clan and other wealthy clans. The males did not want to split the inheritance land while other families avoided the bride prize.

Causes of Female Infanticide in India

Poverty

High poverty and the inability to provide for the children is the primary cause of female infanticide in India. Extreme poverty does not only affect India but other countries like France and England.

Another primary reason for female infanticide in India is to get rid of unwanted children, especially those conceived as a result of rape, the birth of children by unmarried mothers, and deformed children's birth. Lack of a stable income of support couples and postpartum depression have also been reported as causes of infanticide in India.

Dowry

Dowry payment was another factor that contributed to infanticide in India. Some girls were killed to avoid payment of bride prize when they get married. In India, it is a tradition that the bride's family pays the bride's wealth to the groom's family, and sometimes it was too much for the families. For a family with many daughters, this could be a tremendous economic burden; that's why parents got rid of their daughters.

Potential parents' pension

In many homes, children acted as their parent's potential pensions. Parents depended on the children to take care of them when they are old. But in many cultures, the girl leaves her parents and goes to live with her husband. Those parents of boys get more resources when their sons marry, while girls lose their pension. Many poor parents who could not afford to raise large families opted to kill girls and save boys from providing for them when they get old.

Religious beliefs

Some religious beliefs also undermined the roles of women and portrayed men as a superior breed. According to various religions, it was believed that a boy could get rid of all the sins to help you reach god after death. Also, a son-in-law would do the same to their parents- in-law. In many cases bearing a boy was considered prestigious for the father than having a daughter.

The Indian census shows that the sex ratio is low, especially in families with few children, but it gets more balanced as they get more children. The abandonment of sex-selective acts brings about balance. There has been a heated debate on the causes of high population imbalance since some people believe that female infanticide could not be the only cause but natural causes.

Female Infanticide in China

China's female infanticide history goes back to 2000 years. It was used as a means of controlling the population. However, female infanticide was not fully condoned in china. Buddhists believed that killing baby girls would bring bad karma. Those who protected the girls would lead to good karma, which brought a prosperous life, successful sons, and long life. However, the Buddhists believed in reincarnation and convinced the parents that infants' death is not final; this belief helped to ease guilt even after infanticide.

In the 16th century, when Christian missionaries arrived in China, they witnessed children being thrown in rubbish piles and rivers. In the 17th century, Matteo Ricci wrote about the practice he had witnessed in many provinces and attributed it to extreme poverty. The practice went on up to the 19th century but later declined during the communist era. In the census carried out in 1990, the male-female population ratio was 1.66.

In 1980, the one-child policy was introduced in China to prevent population explosion, but it created a large gender imbalance. The policy allowed the parent to carry out ultrasounds and carried out selective abortions to ensure that only boys were born.

Ways we can help eradicate female infanticide:

Female infanticide is a big issue that should be discussed openly and condemned with the strongest terms possible. However, to achieve zero female infanticides requires a lot of effort and patience, but it can be achieved:

Parents should be educated about religious practices that support and empower girls. They should also be encouraged to offer their daughters hand in marriage, which is beneficial to their lives. It is also clear that eradicating the dowry practice could help a lot in curbing female infanticide. Instead of parents worrying about their daughter's bride wealth, they can focus on saving for their education.

Mass education on women empowerment is also a necessary requirement in eradicating female infanticide. Girl education could be the first step to empowering them both intellectually and financially. It is also essential to empower women and encourage them to venture into different businesses to reduce their dependency on men.

Awareness should also be raised that bearing a child is a sign of potency regardless of their gender. Most girls' killings are associated with the fact that girls are inferior to boys. If parents could be made aware of girls' importance, they could consider them future mothers or future great women.

Discourage selective abortions. Most women are using modern technology to know the sex of the child before they are born. In some areas like china, where male children are highly valued, some women opt to abort the pregnancy after realizing the gender of the baby. Women need to be educated on the dangers of abortion and the importance of girls in the community.

Medical family planning is another thing that can help stop infanticide. Women should be encouraged to have the number of children they can manage. The primary cause of female infanticide is poverty. Instead of having a child and killing them later, women would be better encouraged to have a planned family.

Better women protection laws should be put in place. Most women would neglect their children, especially if the child was conceived as a result of rape. Severe punishments should be imposed on rapists and counseling done to the victims to avoid cases of postpartum depression. Also, doctors administering selective abortions should not be spared for their evil deeds.

Authority empowerment: it is also vital to empower the authorities both at the district and state level, to stop the act. If the authorities at the district level could be empowered to shut down female infanticide, it would be easier to trace and stop the act since they are closer to the people than those in authority at the state level.

Female infanticide is an inhuman act that was practiced devaluing women. This practice existed for centuries in different parts of the world. Numerous studies have been carried out to determine the exact number of victims of the vice, but the effort has proven futile. The main reasons for female infanticide were cultural and economical, although some perpetrators blamed it on religion. However, in recent years many organizations and individuals have condemned the vice. It is not easy to eradicate the vice that has been around for centuries, but women empowerment can help reduce it.

CHAPTER 3

Atrocities on women

Like an apple that has fallen from our tree,

my soul is rotting, and I've taken you down with me.

Deep in the emotions of my misery

are the feelings that cannot ever seem to be set free.

You could say others have had it worse than me,

but until you take a few steps in the worn out path of my misery,

with the burdens I've carried, only then can you unravel my mystery.

If only to stumble on shards of glass,

only then to empathize the pain that I stash.

The scars are always there, never to vanish,

never to be repaired.

The physical pain may have vanquished,

but the emotional pain will always lay stagnant in our mind,

always to remind us of our broken home.

The pain we endured through our childhood

made permanent cracks in the building blocks of our foundation, leaving the ones who've moved into our life

to mend the cracks with their love,

to suffer the sometimes bitterness that was left behind,

forever in our minds.

\-   *Rosanna*

In society today, there are several instances of atrocity against women. As a man, how would you feel if it is your sister, wife or even mother being assaulted? The kind of assault concerned with atrocity against women comprises of several aspects. These include sexual violence, intimate partner violence.

Firstly, intimate partner violence, also termed as ex-partner, involves sexual, physical or psychological harm. It includes sexual coercion, physical aggression, psychological abuse and controlling behaviors. Secondly, sexual violence is concerned with any sexual act or an attempt to acquire a sexual act against an individual's sexuality using coercion. It involves rape; which is forceful penetration of the vulva or anus with a penis or any object. There also include harmful traditions that cause more harm than good to women. However, why would you think of exposing women to these atrocities?

Causes

What could be the reason behind the atrocities against our women? The causes of atrocities against women consists of two outlines of analysis; close investigation of the characteristics that influence the offender's behavior and whether some women have an intensified vulnerability to the victimization issue. The atrocities' causal factors are at various levels of analysis, which include institutional, individual, social and dyadic.

The studies carried out on offending and victimization remain conceptually distinct except in the sociocultural analysis whereby the joint consideration is frequently granted to two complementary processes. Firstly, those that place women for the reception of the violence and afterwards operate to silence them. Secondly, those that influence men to be aggressive and pass their expression of atrocities towards the women. There are several single classes of influences that bring about the atrocities against women in society. These include biological factors, for instance, androgenic hormonal influences, theories of evolution and intrapsychic explanations, mostly focusing on personality traits and profile or mental disorder.

Additionally, there are the social learning models, social information processing theory, and sociocultural analyses. Concerning the social learning models, they focus on the socialization experiences that make men practice the atrocities towards women. The social information processing theory concerns the cognitive processes that the offenders tend to engage in before, during, and after the atrocities on women.

Also, the sociocultural analyses aim at understanding the societal structural features at the level of a peer group, family, dyad, state, and media which inspire atrocities against women and render them as a susceptible group of potential victims; and the explanations of feminists emphasizing the gendered nature of atrocities against women and their roots in patriarchal social systems.

Research on the atrocities against women verifies that the atrocities arise from the interaction among the individual psychological and biological factors, and social processes. However, it is not known to what extent is the overlap in the development of atrocities against women and several other violent behaviors. Notably, in the studies conducted concerning the men batterers, it is concluded that several batterers confine their atrocities to their intimates. Some males are also known to be generally violent and practice the atrocities.

In addition, there are harmful societal practices. The practices of these societies work mostly in favor of men and cause harm to the women; for example, there is the rape culture. It became notorious in Brazil following the sexual assault of a 16-year-old girl by up to 30 men. The rape culture involves an environment where sexual violence against women is normalized, and in the media is excused. This culture is geared by the glamorization of sexual violence, objectification of the women's bodies, and the use of misogynistic language. These, therefore, create a society full of atrocities against women.

Women and girls tend to live in fear of being raped, and no one will come to their rescue. What are some of the examples of rape culture in society? It may involve; blaming the victim, trivializing sexual assault (boys will always be boys), use of sexually explicit jokes, and the assumption that only promiscuous women get raped and also teaching women how to avoid getting raped rather than teaching men not to rape.

Consequences

What could be the possible consequences of atrocities against women in society? When faced with these atrocities, women are greatly affected. It could be physically, socially, mentally, emotionally or even psychologically.

Depression

The atrocities against women make them sink into depression so easily. As a human being, women can withstand several life challenges. When faced with atrocities from the male, it disturbs them mentally. Probably due to fear of being criticized for what they have gone through, most women sink into depression. Most women are also depressed when they suffer from chronic illnesses caused by atrocities. They develop trust issues with everyone around them hence cannot speak about what is disturbing them. Therefore, most of them are depressed.

Chronic Health Problem

Due to physical abuse that arises from atrocities against women in society, they may develop long-lasting illnesses. The women can suffer from heart problems, high blood pressure and digestive problems. In the instance a woman is assaulted in any way, they can never forget it easily. The women may lead dangerous lifestyles, which will bring about these sicknesses. They may decide not to take the appropriate meals as they feel betrayed and hurt, so nothing seems meaningful to them. Out of this lifestyle, there arise digestive problems which become a challenge for the better part of their life.

Also, when sexually assaulted, the atrocities bring about the spread of sexually transmitted infections, including HIV. Once one is infected with HIV, it does not have a cure, but it is manageable. These health problems will not affect the women if only the atrocities against women are dealt with.

Unplanned Pregnancies and Unsafe Abortions

In most cases, atrocity against women involves the sexual abuse. It concerns rape in which one forcefully fulfils their sexual desire without the consent of the other party. Once one is involved with the sexual act, they may end up being pregnant. Women have planning on when and which period to sire their children. So, when messed up, they end up having unplanned pregnancies. The women have a number of questions once they realize they are pregnant. These include; will I keep a baby who reminds me of my bad times? Am I ready to have this baby at the moment? What if the child turns out to be a bully like the father? Will I tell the babe he/she was a result of atrocity?

They find the answer to their endless questions as procuring an abortion. They can even seek assistance from quack doctors to terminate their pregnancies. It puts their life at risk as these abortions are unsafe and may have dire consequences for them. Unsafe abortions can lead to damage of their internal organs and also death. Therefore, these atrocities put the lives of women at risk.

Death

Death due to atrocities against women is brought about by several issues. Firstly, physical abuse plays a great role. It may involve a thorough beating on the women, which causes them harm on their body parts. When beaten using any form of weapon, it may miss and hit a sensitive spot, causing immediate deaths. It has been evidenced so many times whereby the women lose their lives due to physical abuse.

Secondly, due to unsafe abortions. When sexually assaulted, it at times leads to pregnancy. Most women are bitter with it and find it hard to keep the baby borne out of atrocity. Due to receiving assistance from non-professional doctors, most of them end up dying during the abortion process. Also, death can be caused by the health-related problems caused by the atrocities. For instance, when the women transmit HIV and fail to take the prescribed medication, they will die within a short span of time.

Possible Solutions

Women are strong pillars in our society who need to be protected. It is your responsibility to ensure that the society does not keep up with atrocities against women. As a society, we need to focus to empower our women and expose them to atrocities that affect them.

So, let's discuss the possible solutions to stem out atrocities against women in our society.

Challenge Rape Culture

It is high time you need to face reality and work against the rape culture. In order to challenge it, you need to speak out whenever you hear someone trivializing rape. For example, saying boys will always be boys when a lady is raped. There is also a need to stop blaming the victim. An individual's dress code is never a good reason for being raped. It is because there are so many women who dress well and end up being raped. To challenge this culture, there is a need to deviate from using language that degrades women in the society.

Listen to Women's Experience with Atrocities

As a society, there is a need to create a conducive environment for women to speak up. Most people criticize the victims of the atrocities terming them to be weak. Therefore, when faced with challenges, the women tend to keep it to themselves. We need to give them an opportunity to speak up about the atrocities. Instead of glorifying the evil acts, we always need to condemn them and at all levels. This will bring back the oneness of people in the society and peaceful living among women.

Create Laws Protecting Women

We need to create laws and enforce those existing laws that protect women. They need to be protected from atrocities including verbal abuse, rape, beatings, trafficking, mutilations and torture. When laws are put in place, any one against them will be charged. Women will be able to report any atrocities against them as they know what is scheduled right for them. The offenders also will not bring atrocities against the women due to fear of breaking the law. Breaking the law calls for punishment and no one is ready to be punished because of mistakes done willingly.

Educate Community Members

There is need to create awareness among the community members concerning effects of atrocities against women. The society should be educated that women are not the only ones vulnerable to atrocities as they are all equal. There is also a dire need to teach them what are the possible consequences of practicing atrocities against the women. On rape issue for instance, the men should be taught not to rape and not telling women to avoid getting raped. They need to understand that rape is not as a result of a certain dressing code. Rapists can go for anyone despite the mode of dressing. It is a societal responsibility to protect women, and hence everyone is responsible.

Summary

In conclusion, atrocities against women have been on the rise. Been attributed to several causes, there is a need to determine what can be the major cause. It involves either a close investigation of the characteristics that influence the offender's behavior or the concern of whether some women have an intensified vulnerability to the victimization issue.

Another cause as evidenced is the harmful cultural traditions practiced in the society. These atrocities, as evidenced, have severe consequences on the women. These include; chronic health problems, depression, death, and unplanned pregnancies and unsafe abortions. The consequences may be long term and may affect the women personally and other people, such as their children.

However, atrocities faced by women need to get a solution. The women deserve better treatment as they play a great role in the society. Some of the solutions that we can put into practice as discussed include; educating the community members to condemn atrocities against women, challenging the rape culture, and listening to women on their experience of several atrocities. Also, we should create laws and enforce laws that seek to protect women from facing atrocities. Therefore, as discussed, we can handle the atrocities that women face. With this, we create a conducive environment in the society where all people are equal; hence unity is promoted.

CHAPTER 4

Raise your Voice

Raise your voice, scream out loud.

Say what you mean, mean what you say.

Your words are you own.

No one can take them from you.

You are your own person, you are someone.

Raise your voice speak out loud.

Make a statement, show that your proud.

So raise your voice and don't be afraid

because you are who you are

and you can't be blamed.

- DeShonda Tyler

Recently, women in America were celebrating 100 years since securing their right to vote. Many may have taken it for granted because 100 years seemed to be a long time ago, but if anything, it is much closer more than you can think.

In almost every country in the world, women are now exercising their rights to vote. Apart from voting, they now need to raise and call for change because there is still more that's needs to be done regarding their rights.

It is high time for women to elevate their expectations in society and speak up their minds. They don't have to accept violence or child abuse anymore. They have to step out of their sense of smallness and gain confidence in owning their power.

In this chapter, we will discuss how women can raise their voice, the benefits of women raising their voice, and why women shy off from raising their voice. Let's dive in!

How Can Women Raise Their Voice?

There are different ways in which women can raise their voice. However, in this chapter; we will focus on the following ways

- o Training girls on the importance of raising their voice at an early age
- o Giving women opportunities to vie for political offices
- o Using ICT to raise the voice of women
- o Addressing the digital divide in ICT
- o Property ownership

1. Encouraging Girls to Speak Their Mind When Young

When girls are young, they have no problem asking anyone what they need. They communicate without hesitation when they are tired, hungry, or when they are generally discontent.

At the age of three, the girl is still confident, and she speaks her mind at home, but one may wonder, will this girl still be confident when she grows up? Will she confidently raise her voice to express her opinion? Will she stand up for others and oppose their oppression?

While the future is unpredictable, a girl expressing herself later in her career is something that most parents, teachers, and coaches cannot afford to leave to chance. That is why girls need to be educated at an early age about the benefits of expressing themselves without fear.

As a teacher, mentor, or coach, here are ways you can encourage a young girl to use her voice for her to develop confidence even when she is grown.

• Ask her

While this may seem obvious, it is an essential technique that most people tend to overlook. What other option do you have other than asking the girl how you can encourage her to use her voice? Once you ask, it is essential to listen to her carefully and take the necessary action.

• Educate her that her voice matters

If you ask most parents or any adult, they will tell you that adolescents-particularly girls have nothing to add to the conversation. That is a gross misunderstanding that parents should avoid at all.

Over the past year, many young girls have proven that their voice matters, and they can make a change. Although the girl may not have a platform on the national stage, she can have her voice at school, home, or in her community. It just a matter of encouraging her, and she will develop the courage needed.

• **Provide an opportunity where she can use her voice**

Most parents fail to understand that, sometimes, all a girl needs is an opportunity to use her voice. For instance, you may start by asking her, "What do you think? And that may be an excellent place to start building confidence in her. Encourage her to think of different scenarios in her life where she can use her voice.

• **Assist her in honing her skills**

With strategies and skills to face a challenge, girls build up their confidence. As you provide an opportunity for your girl to use her voice, also teach her different scenarios where she can use her voice and times when she needs to keep quiet and watch.

Also, let her reflect on situations where she used her voice to address an issue and scenarios where she kept quiet amidst the chaos. What techniques worked for her? What circumstances forced her to use her voice?

Additionally, make it clear to her that using her voice is not always the right thing to do. There is great power in transparency and honest dialogues between the parties involved.

2. Allowing Women to Vie for a Political Position

When a woman participates in politics, there can be a positive impact on the policies made and the type of solutions proposed. For instance, if more women are elected to political offices, more policies will reflect the priorities of the families and women.

Look at South Africa and Rwanda- the moment in these two countries, the increased number of women helped solve land inheritance and reproductive rights. Also, there is likely hood that the high number of women are likely to repeal legislation that restricts women from being household heads.

Therefore, if you feel that the system is oppressing you and you cannot raise your voice, you can run for a political office to change your fate.

3. Using ICT to Raise the Voice of Women

ICTs like mobile phones and the internet can play a critical role in increasing the voice of women. They can also help women to participate in formal and informal public spaces.

Apart from that, women and girls increase their knowledge and information beyond their immediate environment, and they can know whatever is happening on more comprehensive and professional networks. With these new ways of connections, their opinions are heard by different people across the globe.

With ICT, you have an effect where you can raise your voice, attracting supporters and momentum at the same time.

4. Addressing the Digital Divide

While ICT has numerous benefits to political participation and public action, it also has some limitations. There is a vast gender difference when it comes to using, owning, and accessing ICT products.

Fewer women and girls have access to mobile phones and the internet, especially in sub-Saharan Africa. As a result, it becomes difficult for them to voice their problems or discuss other issues affecting them.

In some cases, husbands control how their wives use their mobile phones. Therefore, if it is solved, more women will be connected and can raise their voice towards a common goal.

5. Property Ownership

To boost their self-esteem, women should be encouraged to own property. Policies need to be developed that enables women to own property.

With the property, your social status in society will rise, and you can confidently raise your voice and increase your bargaining power within a household

Benefiting of Raising Women's Voices

Having a voice in any society is paramount. It means that you can raise an issue and be heard. Also, with a voice; you can participate in discourse, discussion as well as decision making. Therefore, listening to women is essential because it enables them to challenge gender discrimination in their society.

Below are some of the benefits that women get when they raise their voices.

Quality Health Care

Quality healthcare matters a lot to girls and women despite where they live, their economic status, or their religious practice. Therefore, their voice is paramount when it comes to health. They need to talk about issues that affect and find a solution to the problems.

With a voice, girls and women progress, and health care accelerates. Nobody can address the challenges and better than the person using the services intended for them-Therefore, involving them is a great move.

Overcoming Violence against Women

Violence against women is one of the greatest human rights violations in the world. Though statistics are staggering, it is reported that one in three women have experienced violence in their lifetime.

You can stop this violence by raising your voice against patriarchy. You can also encourage other women to talk about cases of violence and try as much as possible to help them get justice.

Gender Equality

For years, women have been discriminated against different areas of life. The discrimination starts with the home, workplaces, and particularly in leadership positions.

Women can challenge these discrepancies by raising their voices and fighting for gender equality at work and in society.

Teenage pregnancies

Teenage pregnancies, especially in a developing country, are a huge issue of concern. Such pregnancies can be attributed to the fact that most of these girls lack proper reproductive education.

To make the matters worse, most of these teenagers die while giving birth due to lack of proper medical care. Women can stop such incidences by raising their voices and talking openly about teen pregnancy and how they can stop it

They can up with programs that address early pregnancies and strategies that can be used to solve this problem.

Why are Women Afraid to Raise Their Voices?

If you keenly observe the participants of a meeting with both men and women, you will be surprised to realize that most women don't participate in such meetings. They sit on the sidelines as they observe, others move forward and debate actions to be taken in the future.

However, if you meet the same women outside in a mixed-gender group, they tend to be active with a lot of energy and dynamics. This is so disappointing in many ways, and it should remind us that we have nothing to celebrate as a society.

It's high time we try to find out why women lack the confidence to address issues that affect them.

In this section, we have discussed why women fear talking about issues that affect them.

They fear Ridicule

Most women cannot stand ridicule. They focus on protecting themselves from being the target of aggression.

Speaking about women's rights is not a simple task for many. Therefore, if someone makes offensive remarks on women in your presence, you can raise your voice and stop that person.

Although you may not get support from the crowd, gain confidence, and speak about it even though you are unsure about the consequences. You will have taken a risk that everyone is waiting for someone to take.

They are trapped by their timidity

Naturally, you might be a shy person, and you cannot stand a group of people. You wouldn't like to start any conversation in a group, and you feel you are not a political person.

Although it's not a sin to be shy, you have to gain courage and speak up against women's oppression and discrimination. Don't stay aside and witness other women facing humiliation.

You can make a change in your society by speaking up and letting people rethink who you are.

Temperance

Other women are reluctant to talk about their oppression and discrimination because they don't want to hurt other people's feelings, even though they are on the right track. Most women fail to respond to the issue affecting them with commitment and passion because they are reserved, and they believe that is how women are supposed to behave.

Internet Trolls

Earlier in this discussion, we mentioned that women could use the internet to address their issues. However, it is not easy for outspoken women with substantial social media following because they are likely to be cyber bullied for their advocacy.

Cyber bullying is a new form of violence against women, and most of them cannot face it. Therefore, they tend to shy away from addressing their problems using their mobile phones and the internet.

Conclusion

The women's voices must be heard in their quest for change as women play a critical role in any society. Although legal measures have been put in place to create equality, they are not enough.

More laws and programs must be considered to raise awareness of women's needs. Crucially, organizations that promote women's rights need to be funded to attain effective equality.

Also, women's rights movements must be supported because they also contribute to the quest for women's rights. Most, of these movements' campaign for the right to live without fear of violence and, the right to participate in politics at the highest levels.

CHAPTER 5

Know Your Rights

You cannot rob us of the rights we cherish,

Nor turn our thoughts away

From the bright picture of a "Woman's Mission"

Our hearts portray.

We claim to dwell, in quiet and seclusion,

Beneath the household roof,--

From the great world's harsh strife, and jarring voices,

To stand aloof;--

Not in a dreamy and inane abstraction

To sleep our life away,

But, gathering up the brightness of home sunshine,

To deck our way.

As humble plants by country hedgerows growing,

That treasure up the rain,

And yield in odours, ere the day's declining,

The gift again;

So let us, unobtrusive and unnoticed,

But happy none the less,

Be privileged to fill the air around us

With happiness;

To live, unknown beyond the cherished circle,

Which we can bless and aid;

To die, and not a heart that does not love us

Know where we're laid.

- *Annie Louisa Walker*

Women are entitled to human rights, including protection from discrimination and violence. This helps them enjoy physical and mental health as they are free to vote, own a property, get educated, and earn equal pay.

However, in many parts of the world, women and girls still face gender discrimination. Gender equality, while it has come from far, there are still some gaps that need to be addressed. Gender inequality causes many problems that mostly affect women, including lower pay, sexual harassment, inadequate healthcare, and lack of access to education and public resources.

Women's movements have strived to achieve gender equality by campaigning to change laws or demonstrating on the streets to demand that individuals respect their rights. But, despite their efforts, millions of women continue to experience discrimination. Statistics say that gender-based violence affects not less than 30% of women globally. And those who defend women's rights are castrated and seen as threats to their culture and religion. The integral role played by women in the peace and security of a nation is often overlooked.

For these reasons, it's essential to know your rights if you're a woman. Doing so will help you defend yourself in places you experience discrimination based on your sex.

What Are Women's Rights

These include the entitlements and rights that have been specifically designed to protect women across the globe. Some countries have institutionalized these rights and are supported by behavior, custom, and law. But, in many other countries, women's rights are often suppressed and ignored.

These rights are different from other human rights as they were formed to protect women against violence, biases, and discrimination from men. They're claimed for women and are equal to those of men. Some issues associated with women's rights include sexual violence, right to vote, autonomy, hold public office, enter legal contracts, own property, work, receive equal pay, access family law, and reproductive rights.

Facts about Women's Rights

Many women continue to face discrimination and violence across the globe. The following statistics are an indicator that gender equality is far from being achieved.

- o According to UNODC, 71% of human trafficking comprises girls and women and is mostly for sexual exploitation purposes.
- o UNICEF in 2016 reported that more than two hundred million girls and women in 31 countries have been genitally mutilated.
- o UNICEF in 2018 revealed that approximately 650 million women worldwide were married before reaching 18 years.
- o The United Nations Office on Drugs and Crime reported that 58% of women in 2017 were killed by a family member or a person with who she was intimate.
- o According to the World Health Organization (WHO), 1 out of 3 women worldwide is violated.
- o ILO in 2018 reported that the global gender pay gap was 22%, with women earning approximately 78% of what men are making.
- o The World's Women in 2015 found out that women spend twice as much time as men performing domestic work and when they take up other work, they're underpaid and work for longer hours.
- o More than 80% of women globally aren't protected from discrimination in the workplace according to World Policy Analysis Center.

o The inter-Parliamentary union reported that women make up only 24% of parliamentarians in 2019.

o 1/5 government ministries globally were women in 2019 according to Inter-Parliamentary Union.

Why Is It Important for Women to Know Their Rights?

This modern world is less friendly. It is why human rights have been put in place to help prevent people from taking advantage of others. Therefore, everyone must know how they can protect themselves in case of unprecedented events. Women should know their rights and responsibilities, even if it's on a basic level. You can familiarize yourself with the rights of women by reading materials on the internet or from books in your local library. Here is what happens when women know their rights:

Strengthens the Rights of Workers

Women often work in informal sectors within workplaces that are poorly regulated. This exposes them to not only dangerous working conditions but also sexual violence and harassment. Unfortunately, they only have limited avenues for seeking justice, especially if they're living far from home.

Women face rights abuses every day. They're fired for being pregnant, they're sexually abused by male co-workers, etc. Empowering them with knowledge about their rights helps reduce gender inequalities and creates a society of informed feminists.

They Can Participate More in Political Affairs

Women are now participating in politics as well as leadership. However, those who want to take the leadership role are faced with strong opposition and only have few opportunities. Stereotypes about women's ability to harm those already in power and discourage young girls from pursuing leadership roles in their careers, families, as well as communities. When women know their rights, they can actively participate in political matters as they'll know what to contribute to such matters. Note that women's participation in leadership roles is essential. They'll ensure that laws helping women and other people are implemented, which helps create a better world for everyone.

They Can Challenge Gender-Based Violence

Gender-based violence affects every country. It is, therefore, essential for governments to design improved policies and provide improved services to encourage women who've experienced gender-based violence to seek justice. However, these efforts will be futile if women aren't informed about the laws that have been set to protect them and their rights.

Sexual harassment and other forms of exploitation affect many women. However, statistics report that many of them are yet to understand that they have rights. Sadly, it's not only women living in rural areas, but also those who work in the office. Most rural-based women only understand that they have a right to serve their husbands and stay at home. As such, even if they're violated, they aren't aware that they can challenge that.

Many women stay in dysfunctional marriages because they fear the unknown and fear being victimized for making a choice that doesn't favor their spouse. Knowing your rights as a woman will help you understand violence and report it to the right institutions if it happens.

What Are the Rights of Women?

Right to Education

If women are to participate in civic matters, they need to be educated. Schools help shape people's views towards themselves and those of others. It is, therefore, essential that schools educate learners about gender equality while providing them with a safe environment for learning. The enactment of Title in 1972, gave the right to everyone to access education that's free from discrimination based on one's sex. And since then, women and girls have taken significant steps towards achieving equality, even though some obstacles are still present.

In some places, boys and girls are subjected to different teaching methods in the classroom based on sex-based generalizations. Treating students differently based on their sex is discrimination and the rate at which this trend is growing is alarming. Also, students who are pregnant or parenting aren't treated equally like other students hence most of them drop out.

Students, whether male or female, have equal access to education. And institutions should provide safe spaces for learning to each of them.

Right to Work in Safe and Equal Environments

All women should access equal employment that is free from gender discrimination based on pregnancy, stereotypes, and parenting. While pregnancy discrimination has been illegal for a long time, there are some employees still firing women for breastfeeding or being pregnant.

Individuals should work towards ending discrimination in the workplace and ensure that all employees no matter their race, sex, nationality, disability, or age are paid rightfully as per what they've worked for. Statistics say that women make 78% of what men earn, which is only a 17% increase since the enactment of the Equal Pay Act in 1963.

Right to Safe Abortion and Healthcare

The Roe V. Wade was decided more than 40 years ago by the US Supreme Court that gave women a right to abortion. But, since then politicians and other lawmakers have tried to take this freedom from the hands of the women.

Politicians in some states have been pushing for laws that ban abortion while in others they're shutting the health centers that women rely on for reproductive health services like abortion care. And some, are even trying to end birth control programs, which put women at high risk of unplanned pregnancies.

Although everyone might not feel the same way about abortion, the decision to become a parent or not is private. Politicians should thus stop their interference with women's health care. Sexually active individuals should have access to safe and affordable contraceptives. When women are given the freedom to form intimate relationships, live sexually healthy lives, freely express their sexuality, and decide whether or when to have children, it creates a better and peaceful world.

Right to Safety

Gender-based violence like sexual assault and other forms of sexual exploitation, deny women the ability to live with dignity. Statistics say that sexual violence and sexual assault in women is increasing rapidly. When governments, policies, and laws don't respond to these issues against those subjected to them, they contribute to the devaluation and insecurity of women and girls. Sure, women have the right to safety. However, they cannot ensure that it is upheld on their own. Therefore, governments, landlords, employers, and other actors should be accountable and recognize that discrimination of survivors is also sex discrimination. This will enable women to live in a safe environment free from violence.

Right to Be Pregnant at Work and Come Back to Work after Delivery

A lot of companies especially in developing countries fire women or force them out of the job when they learn that they are pregnant or when they come back to work after delivery. This is especially common in low waged industries that have been dominated by women. In other organizations, pregnant women are denied the same temporary modifications as light-duty assignments, which are given to other employees who need them.

In 1978, Congress passed the Pregnancy Discrimination Act that made it illegal to fire a woman simply because she is pregnant or treating pregnant workers worse than other employees who are also unable to perform some job aspects.

Unfortunately, some employers still do it and even some courts rule in their favor when they come up with a "pregnancy blind" excuse. However, when women are fired from their jobs, they lose incomes as well as benefits. This contributes to poverty and widens the gender pay gap between men and women.

In some cases, some employers fire women as they don't believe that they should get pregnant if they're not married. However, even employers of this kind do not have a free pass of discriminating against the women who choose to be pregnant when they're unmarried.

And even after pregnant women give birth, they still face discrimination when they pump breast milk in the office. Women should understand that they're protected by the law and should speak up against these discriminations that result from being pregnant or giving birth.

How Can You Advocate for Women's Rights?

Educate young girls- activists all over the world are stepping up for gender equality. By educating young girls about the rights of women, we can create a better future for all of us.

Join the conversation- social media campaigns are integral in raising awareness and changing attitudes. Sharing your stories can make a huge difference. Many movements support women's rights, including the "MeToo Movement" and "Times Up movement" in the United States. This helps keep the conversation about gender equality and women's rights going. Everyone is encouraged to join these movements and help bring change.

Sharing work at home- empowering women can begin right from home. Everyone can be involved in cooking, cleaning, fetching water/firewood, or caring for children or the elderly. Note that women usually do 2 ½ times household work more than men. Hence, they have less time to engage in paid labor or work for longer hours. When women take up paid labor, it can sustain families and grow economies.

Support them- if you're in a place that you can make a difference in other women's lives, you shouldn't think twice. Supporting and empowering women is useful in achieving gender equality. You can work with the women to change the legal system or supporting their entrepreneurial work.

Speak Up- an important way of advocating for women's rights is by speaking up, whether a person is talking to their friends or an organization. When individuals raise their voice for the rights of women and gender equality, they can spread awareness, which helps break barriers.

Final Thoughts; What Does the Future of Women's Rights Look Like?

The world is realizing that women's rights are human rights too. And this has bettered the lives of women in many countries. But, in some other parts, women are still treated unfairly and have no rights to protect them. Although women's movements have tried to change situations, it'll take so much effort to create favorable conditions that will help them exercise their rights. While many people know of the existence of women's rights, recognition alone doesn't make it a reality. Nevertheless, with the discussions, movements, and campaigns that are being done, they'll create a safe environment for women to work and live in.

CHAPTER 6

Gender Equality and Equality at Home & Work

she is a daughter, sister and mother

then why always she suffer..?

why we differentiate between he and she

god didn't then why do we..?

this is disappointing everyone not only to me....

to girls we have to give support

give education to them as it works as passport...

now-a-days girls are competing in every field,,,

in army, in airlines and in court...

after getting education named wings,

their flight will land to a bright future.

she may become a doctor, scientist or a teacher....

'he' and 'she' they both have quality,

they both have ability

so we should prefer gender equity and equality....!

-   Shradha

Although in the past decades, there have been progressive efforts to ensure gender equality among men and women in society, there's still some work that needs to be done to address this issue.

Gender equality is among the leading topics in almost every sector. The government, businesses, and employees have worked to equalize issues concerning salary differences between both genders. They've also aimed at ensuring that there is equal treatment between women and men.

In 2015, for instance, 193 UN member countries committed to 17 Sustainable Development Goals, in which goal number 5 was centered on gender equality. It sets ambitions focused on achieving equality while empowering women worldwide by vision 2030.

Five years later, while society has put efforts into ensuring equality, there are still some gaps remaining. Plus, there's some evidence that the COVID-19 pandemic has had some negative influence on gender equality. This chapter talks about gender equality and what can be done to ensure equality at home as well as in the workplace. Read on to learn more.

What Does Gender Equality Mean?

Gender means the social, cultural, and economic attributes that are associated with being female or male. Most communities don't define being a man or a woman in terms of physical or biological characteristics only. Societies have different expectations of how men and women should work, dress, and behave. The relations between genders in the family, at workplaces, or in public, creates a difference in behavior, talents, and characteristics that are appropriate to men and women. Therefore, unlike sex that is purely biological, gender involves both cultural and social aspects.

Gender attributes and characteristics differ in different societies and are subject to change. However, because they're socially constructed, it means that they're likely to change in a way that can make society fairer and just.

Now, gender equality means the right of women and men to get equal opportunities like employment, education, and income to achieve important goals in society while contributing to social, cultural, and political development. It promotes equal pay, freedom from harassment, and discrimination in workplaces whether a person is a woman, a man, married, single, or pregnant. As it encourages equitable advancement of both genders, it is considered an important objective for governments and organizations worldwide that want to establish social and economic structures that will promote development.

Note that gender equality doesn't necessarily mean treating everyone the same. It simply means that their different needs and dreams are valued equally. It is why it is discussed at the same time as gender equity. It addresses discrimination and imbalances in society and ensures that people's rights and access to opportunities aren't different because of their gender.

What Are the Differences Between Gender Equality, Gender Equity, and Women Empowerment?

Gender equity focuses on ensuring that men and women are treated fairly. Society has for so long favored men. Thus, they have many advantages compared to women. Equity, therefore, tries to fill in the women's historical and social disadvantages that prevented them from operating in a fair field.

Equity leads to equality, which creates equal opportunities, resources, and rewards for both genders to ensure that they're both contributing to social, economic, and cultural development. In most cases, women are the ones suffering from gender inequality where they're disadvantaged or excluded from the decision-making process or from accessing social and economic resources.

It, therefore, means that one way of promoting gender equality is by empowering women by ensuring that issues of power imbalances and allowing women to manage their lives are addressed. Women's empowerment is crucial in achieving gender equality. It ensures that decision making, whether at private or public levels, and access to resources is not favored to men. Thus, both males and females can participate equally in productive and reproductive life.

What Is Gender Mainstreaming?

It involves integrating gender concerns when it comes to analyzing, formulating, and monitoring policies, projects, and programs. Gender mainstreaming aims at promoting gender equality in activities that involve development and population. It thus involves addressing men's and women's position and condition in society.

By addressing gender gaps and disparities in areas like division of labor, access to resources, services, information, and opportunities, as well as power distribution and decision making, gender mainstreaming strengthens gender equality values.

However, note that it doesn't just preclude interventions that are focused on only men or only women. Some instances of gender analysis reveal severe inequalities that need sex-specific interventions. But, even in such cases, those interventions should still aim at reducing identified gender gaps by focusing on inequality as the objective instead of the target group. Sex-specific interventions in these contexts are vital aspects of gender mainstreaming. But they should be implemented correctly such that they don't contribute to the marginalization of men in critical areas like sexual health services. Also, they shouldn't contribute to the disappearance of gains or advances that women have already secured instead, they should promote these gains as they contribute towards gender equality.

Why Is Gender Equality Important?

Poverty reduction- research says that poverty rates are higher in girls than boys probably because they don't receive equal education, as well as job opportunities. Gender equality keeps women and their families from being trapped in poverty cycles. When women are given the same education, healthcare, and job opportunities, they can thrive.

Healthier children- when women are allowed to make decisions about their reproductive health, they take good care of the children they have. For instance, when income options are equal to both genders, mothers can provide their kids with healthier food, education, as well as healthcare.

Growth of businesses- if both genders receive equal education and opportunities, they can both contribute towards the development of an organization. Research says that diversities of race, gender, and sexual identity have a positive influence on a company's innovation and productivity.

Better economy- apart from the growth of individual companies, gender equality also impacts the economy. Increasing participation of all genders in the economy, which betters it not just at a country level but also globally.

It leads to better healthcare- according to research women receive worse medical care compared to men. Some reasons for this include lower incomes, lack of education, and sexism in the healthcare system. Even conditions affecting women more than men like chronic pain diseases, aren't well researched. And if they are, they're not taken seriously by the medics. Ensuring equality in women will have a positive impact on their health.

It saves lives- due to lack of empowerment and access to resources, many women face life-threatening risks like natural disasters. If women are given proper education, experts agree that it could save lives, reduce teen pregnancies, and improve child nutrition.

What Is Gender Inequality and What Causes It?

This is when people are given different opportunities due to differences caused by gender issues. It's used when women and men aren't equal because of the biological, cultural, and psychological norms. While it is often discussed as affecting women, gender inequality and discrimination can affect anyone. Some examples of real-world discrimination that relate to the Gender Equality law include;

- o Not promoting a person because of their marital status
- o Making sexual advancement during the recruitment or employment process
- o A vocational training organization refusing to offer cosmetology training to a man
- o Charging women more than men or vice versa for the same services
- o Making sexual comments during the hiring process

- o Denying pregnant girls from accessing education that's equal to their peers
- o Asking workers who are married not to come with their ring at work
- o Male and female workers with the same position receiving different pays even when factors like education level, experience, etc. are similar.

Certain factors directly influence the opportunities given to men and women. Here are some causes of discrimination in genders.

- o Uneven access to education among women and men.
- o Preference for boys when it comes to religious matters.
- o Inequality in employment.
- o Rigid traditions and culture.
- o Job segregations- where men are believed to be better at handling certain jobs than women.
- o Lack of enough empowerment.
- o Lack of legal protections, for instance, against protection from sexual or economic violence.
- o Unequal pay for equal and at times bigger work.
- o Lack of political representation
- o Lack of medical care.

How Can We Ensure Gender Equality at Home?

Gender equality starts at home. Thankfully, many families have taken the steps towards promoting it. Here are ways families can ensure gender equality;

Stop stereotypes, including those you have- gender doesn't just involve biological differences between sexes. But, it's more of a social construct. Society has defined what it means to be a girl or boy and children are expected to conform to this social conditioning, which limits gender expectations and roles at young ages. According to research, children start absorbing stereotypes when they are just three years old, which leads to the world expanding for boys but shrinking for girls by age 10. It is why conversations about gender roles need to start early. Parents need to challenge the attributes and characteristics that have been assigned to women and men at home, school, work, and daily routine.

Encourage your children to speak out- young people worldwide are stepping up for gender equality. When children are empowered and educated about the rights of women, it creates a better future for everyone.

Encourage different role models- children should embrace diversity. Now, role models come in different skin tones, shapes, sizes, backgrounds, and even genders. Parents should encourage their kids to have role models from different genders and ethnicities. Remind them that gender doesn't make a person less important.

Share the care at home- research says that women do at least 21/2 times more unpaid house chores than men. These include collecting firewood, cleaning the house, fetching water, caring for children and the elderly. This has made many of them miss on equal opportunities to go to school, to take a full-time paid job, or have enough time to rest. By equally dividing chores and childcare in your home, you can promote equality. Parents should make sure that they involve both boys and girls in household chores.

Talk about it- by talking to your kids about gender equality and the rights of women, you'll be setting up to lead the way. Make sure that your children know that women and men are all equal. It is also best that parents lead by example.

How Can Employers Ensure Gender Equality in the Workplaces?

Ensure equal pay- this is an important element that all organizations should consider. Salaries should rely on job roles and companies should develop a regular payment structure to improve transparency and remove any salary discrimination. Additionally, employees should be informed about decisions that involve remuneration to avoid any misunderstanding.

Prioritize work/life balance- although the equal pay gap is narrowing among workers, research says that it is widening among mothers who are working as they suffer a penalty when they take some time off. Lack of available childcare support systems is among the issues that limit women from reaching the top of their careers. It's, therefore, essential that companies consider helping in child and elderly care. Additionally, parental leaves for fathers should also be encouraged to relieve working mothers and allow them to invest more time in their professions.

Identify harassment and immediately stop it- many women are subjected to harassment at some point in their careers. Managers, therefore, need to recognize and stop harassment early. Unfortunately, harassment issues are often ignored by many organizations. But it's essential that managers immediately stamp out any harassment issues in the workplaces, no matter how small they are. Companies need to also have policies implemented to stop such issues from happening again. If harassment cases are overlooked, it's an indication that gender inequality is still happening with the company.

Consider leadership roles for both women and men- leadership roles are mostly given to men as society believes that they're better off than women. However, these stereotypes at the workplace cause gender discrimination. If an individual has the right attributes, they should be given the leader's role regardless of their gender. With an adequate representation of women in the leadership roles, many female employees will take up the job opportunities, which ensures the growth of the economy.

Re-evaluate job requirements for senior positions- companies that don't employ women for senior-level roles need to identify the barriers that they've constructed that make them receive fewer applications from women. This does not mean that they must necessarily change the job requirements, but they can question whether truly they need someone with 15 years of experience in management when a person who has 10 years of experience can do the job effectively. Organizations should also determine whether including other experiences will increase the number of applications they get.

Is Gender Equality for Men a Concern?

Gender equality, although mostly centered on women, is also a concern for men. It aims at creating equitable relationships based on the definition of rights for both men and women in all aspects of life including family, workplace, and society at large.

Gender is mostly overlooked as an aspect of a male's identity. That's because individuals consider male attributes and characteristics as the norm while those of women as the variation of the norm. But men's lives just like women are significantly affected by gender.

Society has categorized men as leaders, sons, and husbands. And this has created more demands for them while shaping their behavior. In most cases, men are expected to focus on the family's material needs instead of the nurturing and caring needs, which are women's roles. This socialization at home and school has unfortunately led to some men developing risk taking behavior which is often promoted by stereotyping or peer pressure.

The lifestyle demanded by society for men sometimes results in them being exposed to higher mortality and morbidity risks than women. Such risks include those relating to violence, accidents as well as alcohol consumption. It's, therefore, important that communities encourage men to take up the nurturing role. They also have a responsibility for their child's health and their partner's reproductive health. For these rights and responsibilities to be addressed, society should recognize men's specific health problems along with the needs and conditions shaping them. An important step in creating gender equality in men is adopting a gender perspective since it reveals the disadvantages and costs men face that result from gender difference patterns. It also encourages gender equality not just to be centered on the roles, needs, and responsibilities of women and men but also the relationship between them.

Final Thoughts

Achieving gender equality in all aspects of life is an essential factor for the growth of countries. For governments to create a dynamic and inclusive economy, it must ensure that everyone is given equal opportunities for success. While society has tried to ensure equality, there are still some gaps that need to address. However, if everyone understands that they have a role in ensuring that gender equality is observed, discrimination based on gender might be a non-issue soon.

CHAPTER 7

Empowering Women

A newborn baby smiles

Gazing at her mother

With playful eyes

So innocent

So young

The world is hers for the taking

A little girl laughs

Alone in a silent playground

Her eyes closed

Pigtails whipping through the wind

Without a care

The world is hers for the taking

A young lady cries

Tiptoeing to the edge of the cliff

She has a choice

Irreversible

But she won't because

The world is hers for the taking

A middle-aged woman reads

To a classroom of eager faces

Staring expectantly at her

She prepares to share with

Each and every one

The ultimate power

Knowledge

The world is hers for the taking

A grandmother speaks

Telling her story

To all who wish to hear

She has lived many lives

And in each one she has known

The world is hers for the taking

All these women

Their power

Their ideas

Their stories

The world

Tries to reduce them

To less than their worth

But fails

Because the world

Has always been

And will always be

Theirs for the taking

-   Arshia Agrawal

Critical issues like gender equality and women empowerment are essential for a nation to develop progressively. According to research, when women earn higher salaries, it contributes to better child and family healthcare, which leads to the growth of a nation's economy. Women empowerment has gained much importance among scholars, national as well as international programs. Well, it wasn't until the declaration of the Women's Decade in 1975, that this concept was ingrained deeply into society. But even then, most governments did not accord it the attention it deserves.

But thankfully, governments have started paying a considerable amount of attention to this issue.

Considering women's historically low socio-economic position, it is essential that all organizations come forward to ensure that women are empowered, and their rights are preserved.

Women can contribute to a country's economy significantly. Statistics say that their contribution to waged work in the form of business and labor can boost the economy of a nation. Sadly, in many parts of the world, gender discrimination remains a social issue and these potential women are always affected by poverty, exploitation, and discrimination. But because sustainable economic growth is not possible without women, it is important that they're empowered.

What's WomenEmpowerment?

It can be described as a way of promoting self-worth among women while giving them the freedom to make their own choices and the right to influence social change not only for themselves but others as well. It is closely discussed with female empowerment, which is an essential right that helps create a peaceful and prosperous world.

Empowerment simply means accepting and allowing people to make their own decisions. Women's empowerment is very crucial for the development of a country. It allows women to participate in the political and social decision-making process. Hence giving power to women in society to take charge of their own lives and their communities without feeling discriminated against is women Empowerment.

It involves giving girls and women access to opportunities like education without any restrictions or limitations. Raising the status of women through literacy and training is an important aspect of empowering women. Women empowerment is also a process that allows women to redefine gender roles that have been set by society, which allows them to choose other alternatives that have been otherwise restricted.

The Principles of Women Empowerment

Businesses around the world can develop from equality. The United Nations encourages individuals to use these 7 principles in the community, marketplace, and workplace, which educate society on how to transform women through empowerment. They were developed by a partnership between the United Nations Global Compact and UN Women to support companies in designing or reviewing policies and practices that are aimed towards ensuring gender equality.

Here are the seven principles;

- o Establish a high-level of leadership in organizations that will promote gender equality
- o Treating workers fairly regardless of their gender while respecting human rights and protecting them from discrimination
- o Ensuring the safety of both men and women workers in the workplace
- o Promoting education, training as well as career development in women
- o Implementing marketing and supply chain policies aimed at empowering women

- o Advocating for equality through community initiatives
- o Monitoring and evaluating the progress of policies aimed at achieving gender equality

Men and women should not be treated equally simply because it's the right thing to do, but, because it's also good for business. When women participate fully in entrepreneurship, it helps in the growth of the economy and creates a better future. These principles of guidance help nations ensure fair treatment in all areas, which empowers women and benefits societies as well as companies.

What Are the Components of Women Empowerment?

Women empowerment can be categorized into 5 major components. These are;

- o Freedom of influencing the social change direction, which creates a fair social and economic order both nationally and internationally.
- o Right to have control of their own lives within and outside their homes- women are encouraged to take control of their health and wellbeing as well as other aspects of life. As such, they can make independent decisions regarding their reproductive health, education, etc.
- o Access to opportunities and resources- before, some opportunities were limited to only men. But empowerment is changing the norm. Now, girls can also get a higher education, participate

in economic growth, access to greater health, and political representation. This enables them to reach their full potential while helping meet various international development goals.

o Having a right to determine their choices- it gives them the freedom of making their own decisions in all aspects of their lives, including their reproductive health. Historically, societies established the responsibilities, attributes, and behaviors of women. In most instances, they diminished and undermined them. However, through empowerment, they've been able to decide for themselves how to behave, what to wear, etc.

o Women's sense of worth- It aims at empowering women socially and is among the most prominent empowerment forms usually advertised by mainstream media. It strengthens women's relations and positions in social structures hence giving them a sense of purpose outside their home. It encourages valuing women's contributions to society rather than invalidating them because of their sex. It also fights discrimination by discouraging judgment passed to people from different races, disabilities, religions, and ethnicities.

These components are applied to the economic sphere, which encourages women's economic empowerment by encouraging organizations to expand economic opportunities for women. This strengthens their legal rights and ensures that they have a voice in economic decision making. Nations can expand women's economic opportunities by creating more jobs for them in all sectors and building a climate that supports women from starting and growing businesses and their entrepreneurship skills. Financial institutions need to also provide them with easy access to financial services and products that are tailored to their needs.

Why Is Empowering Women Important?

Better Health for Everyone

Empowering women frees men from the pressure of being the primary wage earner and encourages young men to explore who they are without worrying about the roles that have been traditionally described as feminine or masculine. Hence, they'll have the freedom to take part-time jobs, which gives them the time to bond and interact with their children and do other interesting activities. This creates a free society where everyone can truly be who they want to be.

Additionally, when women get educated and can access resources, they make informed decisions about the number of children to have and how to take care of them. As a result, not only will poverty decrease, but they can provide and cook decent meals for their children.

It is also worth noting that over 80% of agricultural workers worldwide are females. Empowerment, therefore, allows them to buy, grow, and sell crops they want, which reduces malnourishment and increases the food amount available in a country for export.

Growth of the Economy

Women's empowerment allows women to access job opportunities that were otherwise limited to only men. Plus, it eliminates job segregation by allowing them to work in all fields. Additionally, by being empowered financially, it can boost the economic growth of a country, which leads to a nation being more stable while reducing poverty.

It's also worth noting that incredible innovations come from women. For instance, the pee powered generator that was built by a group of girls from Nigeria and the Turkish girl who demonstrated how bananas can be turned into a bioplastic program. Despite facing harassment, women have been excelling in the fields of math and science. If more women are empowered it could lead to more innovations, which ultimately leads to economic growth.

Better Policies and Reduced Risk of Problems Resulting from Being Female

Statistics say that females make up half of the population. Now, since they're the ones who face gender inequality problems mostly, imagine 50% of the world's population suffering from discrimination, assault, and other gender-based problems. Empowering women could help reduce and put a stop to this hence creating a peaceful and prosperous environment for everyone to succeed.

Also, note that since most policymakers are usually men, the needs of women and many other people aren't well addressed. But, when women are empowered to stand in political forums, they create policies that not only save lives but also protect young girls and allow everyone to access healthcare. Women's empowerment is necessary for a better future.

It Saves the Environment

Scientists say that fertility is growing at a rapid rate. And that if the trend continues, the global population could increase significantly by 2081. This will be billions of people competing for food, water, and other resources. However, women's empowerment supports their reproductive healthcare and effective contraception. This will ensure that we stay in a safe healthy sustainable environment. Hence, individuals won't have to worry about fighting for freshwater or food.

How Can We Empower Women Globally?

Discourage Unpaid Labor Work

Women's unpaid labor work is still a big concern about gender inequality. Many times, their labors aren't noticed by society. However, governments can create policies and allocate resources to eradicate this issue. Unpaid labor is a concern for many developing countries and is often associated with low-skilled or rural workers. Society can control factors causing this issue and put measures to protect women from social abuse and violence. This, therefore, encourages them to utilize their potential.

Believe in Their Entrepreneurial Ideas

The one way, nations can reduce gender inequality is by encouraging women to be entrepreneurs. Governments can establish business training centers for women. Most developing countries have an annual budget for women's development. If women are educated and are given equal opportunities for entrepreneurship, it reduces the unequal pay gap hence encouraging women to participate in entrepreneurship.

Mentor Women

Implementing rules alone isn't enough to eliminate gender inequality. Mentoring programs are essential in promoting women as leaders and encouraging them to fulfill their entrepreneurial goals. These programs should employ both personal and professional aspects. While income making skills are important in empowering women, mentoring programs help cater to growing business demands.

Create More Job Opportunities for Women

While women significantly contribute to social and financial development, many of them, especially in developing countries, don't have access to equal job opportunities. Governments can invest in creating decent jobs for women that allow them to grow and develop. It's also important that businesses give equal pay for an equal job. Additionally, companies should encourage women to apply for senior positions by reviewing their requirement policies.

Allocate Leadership and Decision-Making Roles to Women

While many women contribute to the economy significantly, there are still some gaps in gender equality. Sure, women are actively participating in food production, domestic wellness, entrepreneurship, technology industry, as well as energy and climate change. But many women still do not have access to good opportunities and resources that make them qualified for better-paying jobs. Providing leadership opportunities to women and allowing them to participate in decision-making processes will help in empowering them.

What's the Global Landscape of Women Empowerment?

Gender equality is a major topic that forms part of discussions among all sectors. While there are still some gaps, society has come a long way in ensuring that males and females are treated equally. But, although gender equality is a basic right and is crucial for creating a peaceful and prosperous world, many girls and women still face significant challenges worldwide.

Women still don't have enough representation in power and decision-making processes. And in some parts, they still get unequal pay for equal or sometimes more work. Additionally, they face legal and other barriers that limit them from reaching their full potential in their careers. In some developing countries, girls are seen as less valuable than boys. Thus, they're made to do domestic work or married off before they're adults instead of going to school.

Sure, some progress has been made to empower women in several parts of the world. But there is a lot that needs to be done to ensure gender equality.

What's the Role of Men in Women Empowerment?

It is important that men participate in women's empowerment since they're the ones who mostly violate the rights of women in various circumstances like sexual, physical, and moral violence. Therefore, if they do not understand gender equality, women's empowerment won't be possible.

Men play an essential role in achieving gender equality. They can be role models towards encouraging participation in decision-making, creating appropriate working environment, and promoting access to job opportunities. Here's how men can promote efforts to empower women;

- o Participate more in domestic work and family responsibilities
- o Advocate for women's right and access to opportunities as well as education
- o Speaking up about harassment

Final Thoughts

Everyone has a responsibility of empowering women. It starts with showing your support to the women around you by showing them that they matter and they're important. Women empowerment is a team effort that requires the involvement of all humans regardless of their gender.

CHAPTER 8

Diversity and Inclusion

My greatest wish is for humanity

Treating each other with civility

Regardless of each one's ethnicity

All men should be treated with dignity

For when I hear of discrimination

It generates the greatest repulsion

And so as not to create confusion

Every religion deserves inclusion

Judging books by their covers can only bring

More hate, intolerance as hope takes wing

If we could learn to be more accepting

Bells of world peace would surely be chiming

So, join me now in prayer for acceptance

And an end to widespread intolerance

Beyond war there will be a transcendence

Through God's plan we'll live in benevolence

-   Carolyn Devonshire

You have probably heard of the term "diversity and inclusion" several times. As a matter of fact, these two have been hot topics of debate in the past decade. This concept has gained a lot of traction in the corporate world and politics as well. With more people of different genders, races, and ages realizing their potential and rights, it's clear why calls for diversity and inclusion are at the peak.

With so many people talking about these two elements, do we really understand what they mean? Also, what are some of the best practices we can follow to increase diversity and inclusion in an organizational setting? This chapter will answer these and plenty of other questions related to creating a diverse and inclusive environment.

What is Diversity?

Despite being used alongside diversity most of the time, inclusion is a concept of its own. And refers to the achievement of an environment where all individuals despite their gender, race, or age have equal opportunity, are treated fairly, and contribute fully to all aspects of the organization.

Diversity and Inclusion

In most countries, organizations have implemented policies that ensure diversity and inclusion in society. This includes both the private and public sectors. However, the biggest concern is that are these policies really followed. One of the key concerns is the issue of gender inequality. In the 21st century, men still get more employment opportunities than women both at senior and junior positions. Gender and racial stereotypes still persist in the workplace, at home, and society in general.

Is the lack of diversity and inclusion attributed to ignorance or are people still unaware of the merits of these two concepts? This brings us to our next sub-topic, what are the advantages of a diverse and inclusive environment.

Benefits of Diversity and Inclusion

Before we can dig deeper into these benefits, we need to understand that it is our moral obligation to ensure diversity in every organization. An ethical company needs to implement measures that ensure inclusivity within its departments. Below are other benefits;

- o Gender and ethnically diverse companies are likely to yield more revenue. We live in a diverse world and therefore, for an organization to understand its audience, the workforce needs to be diverse as well. Because every gender or race has a unique trait that they bring to the table, it will be easier for the company to meet customer objectives.

o In some countries, organizations that ensure diversity and inclusion especially in senior positions enjoy tax relief.

o Most organizations that have a diverse workforce are performing better. For instance, it is evident that companies with women as CEO's are doing so much better than with their male counterparts.

o Employees prefer and feel more comfortable when working in an inclusive work environment. Imagine you are a woman and on your first day at the office, everyone working around you is a man. Not only will this look weird, but you may not fully explore your potential.

o Clients love diverse companies. Contrary to general opinion, society has realized the relevance of diversity and inclusion. Because of this, they are willing to support companies that follow this approach in recruitment. Therefore, adopting these concepts is likely to help your company attract plenty of new audiences and clients.

o Diversity and inclusion boosts employee productivity and morale. Being part of an inclusive workforce makes you feel enthusiastic about work.

Statistics Related to Diversity and Inclusion

According to research done by Glassdoor in 2014, 67% of job seekers prefer to work in an inclusive workplace environment. And at least 50% of current employees want their organization to improve their diversity and inclusion efforts.

To prove how determined the society is about diversity and inclusion, in the past year, Gallup found out that 45% of Americans experienced some form of harassment and discrimination due to their gender, race, and age.

Culture Amp, in their recent research, discovered that only 40% of women are contented with the decision-making process at their place of work. This means that the majority feel left out and can't voice out their opinion.

In a study conducted by the Harvard Business Review, 78% of employees agreed to work with an organization that lacked diverse leadership positions. This implies that their leaders are most likely men. The dangers of working in such an organization is that an employee can lack morale, for the female staff there is no role model to look up to and this is likely to slow down progress in the company.

Fast Company identified that a higher representation of women in C-suite level positions guarantees a 34% increase in profits. This is an evidence that women in power ensure organizational success.

Ways to Improve Diversity and Inclusion

From the above statistics, it is clear that we still have a long way to go before we can achieve inclusion in our society. Yes, there are policies in place but are they really executed? Probably not. Learning to speak up to our executives on matters of diversity and inclusion will ensure that changes are made. If we keep quiet, then affected parties will suffer the consequences the most. Other than that, below are ways on how we can improve diversity and inclusion;

Create and Implement an Inclusive Workplace/Organization Model

In the organization you operate in, do you have an inclusive workplace model? You don't have to be part of the Executive Management, for you to know this answer. You just have to look at the surroundings and know whether you are a diverse workforce. For example, is there gender equality in your leadership? Is the managerial board full of only men? Do you work alongside different races? Does your Muslim colleague feel comfortable about making his daily prayers within the premises?

These are all matters that need to be addressed immediately. Inclusion is all about equality and fair treatment. And if your organization lacks that then you do not have a diverse workforce. No one has to hide part of their identity for them to be accepted in the society. If a woman is breastfeeding, the company needs to set aside some privacy for her to perform motherly duties before returning to work.

Does Your Executive Portray Diversity and Inclusion?

Reforms should always come from the top. If there is no diversity at the senior level, how can you expect it to be implemented in other departments? Walk into any company today and there is an 80% chance that the manager or CEO will be a man. To enhance diversity and inclusion, the human resource department ought to enforce these concepts in the organization. Recruitment should be fair and not gender biased.

Acknowledge Social and Cultural Practices

Because we are all different, no belief or practice should be superior to another. An organization should acknowledge all social and cultural practices. Does your company have a football team that plays every weekend? Instead of it being a man's affair, involve the ladies as well, both on and off the pitch.

And it's not just about co-curricular activities. Aspects such as religion and culture should be accorded the respect they deserve. All holidays need to be celebrated equally. Organizations can opt to make holiday parties nondenominational so that no one feels left out.

Ensure every Voice is Heard and Respected

Just because you are a woman working in an office surrounded by men, that doesn't mean your voice should be silent. Yes, some religions advocate for submissiveness amongst women. But we are in the 21st century. What a man can do, a woman can do better.

To enhance respect in society, everyone should speak up and be heard. Organizations should encourage such practices in their offices and as a result, employees will feel safe and contented. Policies put in place should enforce non-discriminatory practices. Those found guilty should be punished.

Encourage Dialogue about Gender Equality

If diversity and inclusion haven't been part of your company's objectives, then the first and most important step is encouraging dialogue about these topics. Through dialogue, the issues surrounding inclusivity will be addressed and solutions can be sought after.

For instance, if there is no gender balance, through dialogue we can identify why that is happening. If the HR is at fault, then they can be reprimanded and advised to be gender-sensitive during recruitment. Should the issue of gender pay inequality pop up, employees can communicate their grievances and ensure everyone is paid equally depending on their contribution to the company.

Promote Diverse Thinking

Yes, you may be successful at recruiting a diverse workforce, but if you don't promote inclusivity then it's easy to lose all those talented individuals. Once you launch diverse policies in your organization, start promoting diverse thinking. You can kick things off by allowing different dress codes depending on culture, including religious holidays on the company's calendar and doing any other thing that creates a diverse environment.

Build a Multigenerational Workforce

Even though it takes experience for one to reach the top, an inclusive workplace environment should feature a multigenerational workforce. The board of managers shouldn't only be composed of senior people. The young generation has a lot of things to offer an organization. They are fast, tech-savvy, brilliant, and very professional when it comes to executing work-related matters.

With such a workforce integrated into your organization, there will be no huge backload. And with the older generation still around to offer guidance and mentorship, a company can succeed beyond its expectations.

Make the Workplace Inclusive

Last on our list is that companies need to make their workplaces inclusive. The work environment needs to be gender and cultural friendly. Mothers need not hide in a conference or washroom when pumping milk. There need to be rooms dedicated for this purpose. The rooms should be well ventilated, equipped, and with covered windows for privacy. This is just but an example of how workplaces can be made inclusive. Another example that can be used is setting aside a prayer room for Muslims.

The more approaches used in improving diversity and inclusion, the sooner an organization can start enjoying the benefits of these concepts. Those in charge should focus on igniting debates and discussions related to diversity and inclusion.

How to Develop a Diversity and Inclusivity Initiative

Now that you understand the benefits of diversity and inclusion, as well as ways you can improve these concepts in the society, let's finalize with how to develop an inclusion and diversity initiative.

1st Step – Data Compilation

The organization needs to know their employee data so that it can be evaluated on the scales of inclusion and diversity. This means looking at age, gender, family status, ethnicity, and other demographic data.

2nd Step – Point Out Areas of Concern

From the data, areas that lack diversity need to be pointed out. If the leadership is only full of men, then that needs to be pointed out. Other aspects such as Asian, Black, Hispanic, and White representation also should be evaluated.

3rd Step – Address These Issues by Implementing Policies

Policies should be created and implemented to solve the above concerns. For instance, organizations may start limiting their employee referral programs if the labor being sourced is of a particular race, gender, or age. The company can set up measures aimed at curbing unconscious biases in the office.

4th Step – Communicate Initiatives

These initiatives put in place need to be communicated to all members of different departments. This will make it easy for the policies to be adopted. Newsletters, emails, and even flyers can be used. The organization may also decide to include these efforts in its company magazine and create awareness.

5th Step – Measurement of Results and Making of Adjustments

The final step involves an analysis of the outcomes and making adjustments on sectors that need rectification.

The Bottom Line

Diversity and inclusion should be a company's top objectives and missions. It is our moral obligation to treat everyone equally and that can be achieved through promoting these concepts. Above is a strategy the company can follow to create a diverse and inclusive environment. Don't forget that adhering to these measures gives your organization a competitive advantage.

CHAPTER 9

Women in Leadership

I am a striving woman leader and I want to make things fair

Women are more than cooks, cleaners, sex appeal, and childcare

We need to appreciate women we are smart and deserve to be respected

Stop listening to societal norms those need to be rejected

Until we are treated equal, I won't be satisfied

Go sit at the head of the table you are more than qualified

- Haley Sawyer

For years, females have had to battle gender inequality both in the workplace and at home. However, despite all these efforts, women remain underrepresented in leadership roles and positions. Stereotypic gender role expectations remain to be the leading cause of this anomaly.

Women have proven that they can take on leadership roles in different sectors and succeed. It is high time that leadership adopts a gender-neutral perspective and the society breaks free from traditional ways of thinking.

Today, we have women leading in different sectors such as politics, education, entrepreneurship, health, and even complex industries such as engineering. These top roles being scooped by women are at international, national, and regional levels. This proves that gone are the days when only a man would head an organization, company, industry, or even country. The internet is full of success stories on how women are changing the world through leadership.

There is no denying that in these modern times, women have evolved significantly and are reaching milestones that no one thought would be possible. The likes of Oprah Winfrey, Kamala Harris, Nancy Pelosi, Sheikh Hasina Wazed, Queen Elizabeth II, and Mingzhu Dong are living testimonials that women can lead successfully and make uncountable achievements as well as contributions.

With that being said, in this discussion on women in leadership, we are going to define who a leader is, the characteristics they should possess, the reasons why women make great leaders, and why the world should commit to placing more women in positions of power.

Definition of Leadership

Every group, company, or organization needs a leader to manage, oversee, and execute key functions. An organization without a leader is likely to plunge into chaos. This is the same for a country without leadership, it will probably turn into anarchy and later become inhabitable.

A leader can be defined as an individual who possesses a superior position and is tasked with the role of influencing others to achieve objectives. The label 'leader' isn't gender specific. Instead, there are qualities that make one a leader. Therefore, both women and men can be chosen as leaders provided, they showcase their ability and strength to become one. Kindly note that even though these two genders have different styles of leadership, none can be termed as more superior than the other.

Features that Determine Good Leadership

- *People-Oriented* – Remember, a leader is in charge of a group of people. Therefore, a key quality they must possess is being social, expressive, and able to establish close ties with those they are working with.
- *Cooperative* – Not unless the goal is to dictate, a leader should cooperate and relate well with everyone even the most subordinate staff. Cooperation leads to teamwork and orderly execution of commands.
- *Capable of Multitasking* – A good leader ought to have the capacity to operate in different fields and do so at the same time. No matter the size of an organization, chances are there will be different departments. None should be left unmanaged.
- *Emotional Prevalence* – Showing empathy and practicing inclusivity are some of the key things that make a good leader.
- *Being Prone to Change* – Everything is destined to change. Leadership requires one to have the strength to accept and adopt new changes.

- o Other traits include; encouraging participation, sharing power, providing support and assistance.

From the above requirements of what makes a good leader, it is evident that women possess more qualities. Below we are going to prove this to you by showing why women make great leaders.

Reasons Why Women Make Great Leaders

Use a Transformational Leadership Approach

Women leaders tend to be more transformational than their counterparts. At the workplace or home, a woman leader is likely to be the role model of their juniors. They inspire, motivate, and nurture young talents. Instead of only focusing on meeting objectives, women leaders work to transform and better those that they work with.

Task-Focused and Objective Oriented

From time immemorial, women have always been focused on the completion of tasks. This is a skill that is essentially needed in an organization. For things to run smoothly in a company, tasks must be completed before deadlines and all objectives ought to be met within the stipulated time frame.

Promote Collaboration and Cooperation

This trait is heavily attributed to feminine characteristics. Women when in leadership positions, you will find them advocating for collaboration in the organization. This cooperation goes a long way in seeing that different departments use their strengths to meet the overall objectives of a company.

Encourage Participation

Men are well known for their command and control style of leadership. Whereby you find everyone dancing to the tunes of the boss and failure to which, you risk losing your job. On the other hand, women encourage participation. Or more to say, they prefer a democratic style of leadership. Everyone gets a say at the table and this allows room for development in the organization. Through participation, a company may source brilliant ideas and concepts which will contribute to success.

Healthy Competitors

It is a fact that women are more modest than men. And if it's competing with colleagues or other companies, women understand the limits one has to constrain themselves to. Women in leadership steer their organizations towards ethical practices.

Highly Value Work-Life Balance

To most women, balancing between work and life is of the utmost importance. They possess both personal and professional skills. As a result, it is easier to approach a woman leader with an off request and get a positive reply. Due to their appreciation of life to work balance, women are likely to understand when an employee needs some time off.

Women are empathetic

A good leader should be respected not feared. Since women are empathetic, there is a higher chance of them gaining the respect of their subordinates, instead of instilling fear. Through empathy, women can motivate, inspire, educate, and become mentors. Thanks to empathy, women don't hesitate when sharing knowledge and skills that can help others become better.

Excellent Listening Skills

Unlike men that rush you through a discussion, women prefer to listen and evaluate the information being communicated. They appreciate what is being said and digest vital points while making corrections. For the sake of the success of an organization, a leader must have excellent communication skills.

And due to their possession of excellent communication skills, women leaders are very clear when allocating tasks, chairing meetings, and addressing problems affecting the organization.

Ambitious and Dream Big

It is in their nature for both girls and ladies to be ambitious and dream big. To prove this, call a little girl and ask her what she dreams of. You will be amazed at how big most women dream. And as if that's not enough, they are very ambitious towards achieving the said dreams. This ability can see to it that the dreams and objectives of a company are met.

Great at managing Crisis

In an organization, crisis is inevitable. Women, especially mothers have been handling crises ever since their kids were born. These are years of experience in crisis management. This is a skill that very few men possess. And to make matters even better, women's crisis management skills feature patience and compassion. Therefore, the odds of things getting out of hand are next to zero when a woman is in charge.

Getting Women in Leadership is Crucial

A woman will defy the odds to ensure her organizational succeeds. And they will not stop till they soar as high as possible. Any institution, be it a company, industry, or even a country, can't thrive without including women in leadership positions.

All the above qualities that women possess helps create a different perspective on life. They see things from angles that men wouldn't. As you are reading this chapter, organizations that are being led by women are succeeding in so many ventures. And it would be imprudent if an organization would ignore the role of women in leadership.

Thanks to their abilities to empathize, mentor, collaborate, and connect with others, a group led by a woman can establish itself and create a sustainable future. Not to mention, recent statistics show that companies led by women generate more revenue.

Representation of Women in Leadership

Having seen how beneficial a woman leader is, why don't we evaluate how far we have gone in terms of workplace gender equality?

In the past 5 years, we have seen a drastic rise in women's leadership. But, basing our argument that women leadership started from a mere 1%, there is a lot of work that has to be done. According to the United Nations, the following are figures indicating the percentage of women in leadership positions;

o Only 11 women are serving as heads of states in the world.
o 24.3% of all national parliamentarians are women. And it is only in three countries where women are more than men in Parliament.
o The UN has also noted that countries involved women in leadership ended up making political decisions that positively impacted their country.

Moving on to the economic sector, according to a study done by Pew Research, only 5% of CEOs of major corporations in the US are women. This only tells you how little improvement there has been in advocating against gender inequality. On the bright side, however, 44% of the companies in the US have at least three women occupying managerial positions.

The new service economy doesn't rely on physical strength, instead, skills, critical thinking, and the ability to make decisions are the main factors one should consider when offering employment. Living in an era where the economy is terrible, a female brain which is usually wired towards creating a sustainable future and build the society can be of immense assistance.

Challenges Faced by Female Leaders and How to Overcome them

As much as we are campaigning for women to get in leadership, the truth of the matter is that the few who are already occupying these positions are not having an easy time. Working as a leader in a society that thinks you are not fit to be one is likely to cause so many challenges.

They include;

Being Held to Higher Standards

Compared to their male counterparts, women are held to higher standards. For them to be accepted as leaders, they need to do more, and this can weigh them down both professionally and in their personal lives.

To overcome this hurdle, women have to learn how to speak up. None of your achievements should go unnoticed. Flaunt them as much as you want and never let anyone pull you down. Never be a victim of double standards.

Gender Stereotypes

Though a thing of the past, gender stereotypes continue to infiltrate our society. For instance, take a leadership position such as heading a sports team. Most people would say that a man is more qualified for this position. But, why not a woman? Should women focus on lighter duties such as managing a retirement home or hospital?

These stereotypes need to be stopped. Women have extraordinary abilities and can excel in any field. The more women engage in an activity, the sooner it becomes normal for the society. So, don't let anyone hold you back. Go for that leadership position even if it's mostly handled by men.

An Uneven Playing Field

Even if you manage to ace that CEO position, men have what they would like to call "numbers". In that, they turn office work into chess, whereby they source votes before meetings and dictate positions of board members.

Though a challenge, there is nothing wrong with playing dirty at the office. You too can pocket a few board members so that you can have things go your way. Play the same game as they are.

Having Many Roles

Other than being a leader, a woman is also a mother and wife. These other occupations also have tasks that need to be done. As a mother, you are supposed to take care of your child, feed them, and make time to go for their football game. All these things need to be done and you also have to work.

Learn to plan your schedule. Don't do too much of one thing and forget the other. Make time for work, family, friends, and yourself. After all, you do need breaks and vacations regularly.

These are just but some of the few challenges that women in leadership go through. Others include harassment and lack of mentors. As a strong and smart woman, you need to find solutions to these challenges. Never let someone harass, intimidate, or scare you. Speak out and be bold. Also, never look the other side. Because if we don't fight for change, who will?

Dear Women, Don't Take Your Foot Off the Pedal

Being a woman and a leader isn't easy. There are so many challenges we are going to go through before we realize gender equality. Never stop looking for ways on how you can add value to your life and career. If a CEO position opens up and you have got the skills, send in your application. Does your local football team need a manager? What are you waiting for? Women are born leaders, and the society needs to be aware of this.

CHAPTER 10

The Role of Men in Women Empowerment

"When women are empowered, they immeasurably improve the lives of everyone around them—their families, their communities, and their countries. This is not just about women; we men need to recognize the part we play too. Real men treat women with dignity and give them the respect they deserve."

-   Prince Harry

When it comes to campaigns for pushing for women's empowerment or gender equality, a lot of attention is given to women, either by training or mobilizing them. But, while so much focus is given to women to help them, society sometimes forgets that involving men is an integral contribution towards women's empowerment. Women face structural discrimination like gender-based violence. This can only be handled effectively if men are actively involved in putting a stop to it. Men need to be fighting alongside women instead of reinforcing patriarchal norms.

Much discrimination that women face is linked directly to their relations with men, especially when it comes to access the resources and decision-making. Experts, therefore, agree that it's almost impossible to address the challenges and constraints faced by women without involving men. Women from all over the world continue to receive lesser pay compared to men for the same work. And in many parts, they don't have rights protecting them to property, land, inheritance, access to credit cards, and other resources. Changes in these areas will affect men therefore will require their involvement in those changes.

Men still dominate the decision-making process in all areas worldwide. Women's representation in key areas like the judiciary, media, academia, economics, and decision making is still low. Additionally, equal sharing of responsibilities at home between men and women remains a serious impediment to women empowerment and prevents women from accessing benefits like education, employment, political participation, etc. While it has been addressed as a vital issue in many places, for instance, the Platform for Action adopted in 1995 in Beijing, little progress has been witnessed. It is, therefore, evident that without the participation of men in empowering women, efforts to fight for equality will be futile.

What Role Do Men Play in Empowering Women?

Ending Violence against Women

Male violence is not only a violation of women's human rights and freedom, it also obstructs them from fully participating in social and economic life and prevents the efforts towards women empowerment. It expresses domination and discrimination against women as well as unequal power relationships between males and females that have historically been observed.

Violence includes many forms such as pornography, sexual harassment, prostitution, rape, trafficking, and sex-related acts. These acts are committed by men to women to hurt, degrade, discriminate, and silence them from taking control of their own lives, situations, and in extreme cases, kill them.

Men have a responsibility to ensure that they don't violate women and speak up against violations. Some policies have been implemented to address male violence against women. These include perpetrator programs for men who are violent to women.

Additionally, society has put in place measures that end men's practices of buying women's bodies. Prostitution and trafficking in women are today seen as violations of their human rights. A major factor contributing to prostitution and other forms of sexual exploitation is patriarchal ideologies, which give men the right to buy women's bodies. It's, therefore, essential that men and boys change their behavior to help stop the sexual exploitation of women. Policymakers must stand against women's sexual exploitation by challenging those who demand this service, that is, male sexual service buyers.

Ensuring Equality in Workplaces and at Home

Women have been assigned care and domestic work historically while men have been considered breadwinners for the family. Although this is trying to change today, efforts are slowed by public policies, religious beliefs, traditions, stereotypes of gender, and conservative education.

Societies need to encourage a culture where men and women are considered as actors and cares. It is why policies should be established both at home and at work to help break inequalities. Organizations can help support equality by allowing paternal leaves to fathers and avoiding policies that discourage work division and promote traditional gender roles like fixed low benefits for home cares.

Additionally, men should do away with their stereotypes about gender roles in the home. Also, society should encourage men to pick careers and educational programs that are currently women-dominated.

Ending Stereotypes of Gender

This is a lengthy process that must be achieved by public policies in all areas. But, even at individual levels, men can still break these stereotypes. For example, sports are a male-dominated area from athletes, coaches, spectators to consumers. Encouraging both boys and girls to be involved in sports at early ages can help empower women.

Also, the media can help break stereotypes by promoting other images of women and men that are based on equality. For example, it should prohibit sexism and include women in the decision-making process in the media.

Allowing Women to Make Decisions about Their Reproductive Health

Many women worldwide are denied control over their bodies while they're young and even in their adult lives. In most cases, men determine women's sexual experiences and reproductive life, which often denies women the opportunity to a safe and satisfying sexual life. It's thus essential that men's sexual practices and behaviors be addressed to foster an equal relationship between men and women.

Sexual education programs for both boys and girls should be put in place to educate them about their sexual behavior and gender identities. These programs should include a no-tolerance policy for male sexual violence against women. Also, men must be at the front line in pursuing and convicting male perpetrators of sexual violence to signal others that this is unacceptable behavior.

Where Men Are Currently at in Supporting Women Empowerment

Over the past years, the crucial role that men play at home, workplace, and community in promoting women empowerment has been widely recognized. Achieving women empowerment has been acknowledged as a societal responsibility that requires full participation and partnerships from both women and men. There's increasing research relating to men and gender equality. Many academic journals have been written, research conferences have been held, and internal literature focusing on the role of men in gender equality is still growing.

Initially, efforts aimed at understanding the role of men in women's empowerment and increase their participation in this issue, largely focused on men as the ones discriminating and harassing women. It's why policies and advocacy programs that aimed at changing men's attitudes and behaviors were designed to improve women's position in society.

But as more men have come out to stop violence and actively empower women, the focus has shifted to the important role men play as allies and partners, which contribute to building a just society. Their support for equality has been noticed in advocacy, campaigns, and education programs for boys. These have challenged the gender stereotypes encouraging men to take roles that were previously considered for women. Committed men have taken leadership in increasing awareness of the benefits of women empowerment for themselves and society at large.

Areas That Need Improvements

Although the participation of men in empowering women has increased, there are still some areas that need change. These are:

Sharing responsibilities of the family

There's a need to increase men's participation in domestic work and family responsibility. This can be achieved by encouraging a working life for both men and women by adopting policies and programs that support this. Both men and women can gain so much from being closer to their children and participating in the family. Unfortunately, work-life imbalances make these almost impossible.

Although in many countries' women can access employment opportunities, men have not increased their participation in domestic responsibilities. No matter how much women are involved in paid labor, they're still the ones who mainly do domestic work, childcare, care for the elderly, disabled, or sick family members. The increase in the number of older people and HIV/AIDs infected people who need care has made this difficult for them.

If more men are encouraged to participate in family responsibilities and home care, they'll promote women's empowerment. Society should do away with cultural and institutional barriers that make it hard for men to fully engage as fathers and designed practices, as well as policies that allow individuals to share responsibilities. Some of the things that can be done include ensuring family-friendly measures like paternal leaves, flexible working hours available to both women and men, and ensuring an equal gender pay for equal work.

Men as advocates of change in the workplaces

Nowadays, women have entered into the labor market and families in different parts of the world are now depending on the earnings of both men and women. However, workplaces can be major places for gender inequality and discrimination against women. Because men are still the key participants in decision making, they have a role in promoting the economic rights of women as well as their independence. Men should actively participate in putting a stop to harassment while ensuring that women can access employment within appropriate working conditions.

What Barriers Affect Changes

Although men's involvement in empowering women is critical, studies say that it won't be easy. Some of the barriers that affect men's full participation include;

Resistance from men

Even though everyone will benefit from women's empowerment, research says that men's support of this issue begins from an ethical level. Therefore, they should first feel morally obligated to take actions that'll empower women. But unfortunately, although there are many examples of men supporting equality, there is still some resistance. Many of them need to be persuaded that they will benefit from women's empowerment.

Resistance is because society has made them believe that they benefit from the current gender order in terms of power and resources. Also, note that society associates masculinity with being strong and the breadwinner. As such, some men may deny women employment and career development as they are protecting their status.

But, while there is some resistance, it's essential to remember that men aren't homogeneous and can be mobilized to support policies that empower women.

Opposition from women

Opposition comes from women who fear that men might take the leadership of what has always been a women's movement. Others also fear that men's attention may distract resources from women's empowerment.

What's the Way Forward?

The best way forward is to increase awareness of the disadvantages that the current gender order has to both women and men and highlight how changing it will benefit them all. It's thus important that we identify and address the stereotypes of both genders, including masculinity concepts. When men understand the prevailing stereotypes and how they influence their attitudes as well as behavior, effective policies can be established to increase their roles in empowering women.

Various actors who influence boys' and girl's perceptions of being a man or a woman should be engaged to promote a new gender order. Changes in socialization will be easier when they begin at an early age when attitudes and behaviors that shape one as a woman or man are being formed. Families, schools, mass media, and male-dominated areas like sport groups should all be involved in promoting women's empowerment.

Let's Get United in Achieving Women Empowerment

When both men and women work together, gender equality and women empowerment will be achieved sooner. If they treat each other as adversaries instead of allies, we will never move forward. Men and women aren't interchangeable, but men can embrace the unique strengths of women and treat them right. Companies with more women can leverage their strengths to benefit the growth of the organization. For instance, women are generally compassionate and are involved in community building. These traits can improve the behavior of male coworkers. Some things that men can do to support women empowerment include;

- o Listening to them, hearing their stories, and trying to understand their experience with curiosity and compassion.
- o Advocating- male advocacy for women empowerment is valuable and essential.
- o Engage-often men worry that when they engage in gender issues, they might say something offensive or be seen as sexist. Therefore, they shy from saying or doing anything. However, although this issue might be uncomfortable, it's essential to engage and keep in mind that women empowerment isn't just a woman's issue but rather a human issue.

Different Male Centered Strategies That Will Promote Women Empowerment

Gender-based strategies focus on both men and women to help fight the unequal power relationship between them and help end gender inequality. Societies can employ these strategies to ensure men are actively involved in empowering women;

Focusing on gender relations- this strategy addresses the inequalities between men and women by working with both genders. It increases awareness of the gender construction process, which leads to the dismantling of the unequal relationships between men and women.

Raising Awareness among Men- it focuses on boys and men and aims at increasing men's awareness of themselves and their gender. This is a crucial strategy as it helps them understand that women's empowerment wouldn't be a threat to them.

Partnership Approach- This is based on understanding that men and women should work together to ensure equality. It helps men understand that they'll also benefit from women's empowerment. But sometimes this approach has proven to be consensual, which makes it difficult to address issues of power, access to resources, and men's violence against women.

Final Thoughts

Women empowerment is still to a large extent considered a women's issue. But individuals should understand that this is a societal issue that concerns everyone regardless of their sex. Men and boys, like women and girls, need to understand the importance of women's empowerment and the roles they can play in promoting it. Since men are still key decision-makers and economy, organizational power, and public resource holders, they have a responsibility of identifying and ending discrimination. Although there's a great understanding of gender equality in men today, a lot still needs to be done to change the attitudes and behaviors of individual men towards this process.

References

1. https://www.undp.org/content/undp/en/hom
   e/presscenter/pressreleases/2015/05/06/wome
   n-still-earn-24-percent-less-than-men-20-years-
   on-after-two-decades-of-concerted-efforts-to-
   boost-women-s-rights-reducing-poverty-among-
   women-and-girls-remains-critical-for-
   development-progress-say-officials-at-global-
   women-s-conference-.html
2. https://en.wikipedia.org/wiki/Female_infantici
   de_in_India
3. https://en.wikipedia.org/wiki/Female_infantici
   de_in_India#:~:text=In%202000%2C%201%2C
   218%20cases%20of,child%20sex%20ratio%20(C
   SR).
4. https://www.unodc.org/unodc/en/frontpage/2
   016/December/almost-a-third-of-trafficking-
   victims-are-children_-unodc-
   report.html#:~:text=Additionally%2C%20wom
   en%20and%20girls%20comprise,on%20Trafficki
   ng%20in%20Persons%20states.
5. https://data.unicef.org/topic/child-
   protection/female-genital-mutilation/
6. https://www.unicef.org/rosa/press-
   releases/unicef-report-over-half-billion-
   uncounted-children-live-countries-unable-
   measure-sdg
7. https://www.unodc.org/documents/data-and-
   analysis/GSH2018/GSH18_Gender-
   related_killing_of_women_and_girls.pdf

8. https://www.who.int/news-room/fact-sheets/detail/violence-against-women#:~:text=Global%20estimates%20publis hed%20by%20WHO,violence%20is%20intimate %20partner%20violence.
9. https://www.ilo.org/wcmsp5/groups/public/---dgreports/---dcomm/---publ/documents/publication/wcms_650553.pdf
10. https://www.ilo.org/global/about-the-ilo/newsroom/news/WCMS_008091/lang--en/index.htm
11. https://www.un.org/sustainabledevelopment/blog/2015/09/historic-new-sustainable-development-agenda-unanimously-adopted-by-193-un-members/
12. https://link.springer.com/referenceworkentry/10.1007%2F978-3-319-70060-1_15-1
13. https://www.glassdoor.com/employers/blog/diversity/
14. https://www.gallup.com/workplace/215939/invest-diversity-inclusion.aspx?utm_source=link_wwwv9&utm_campaign=item_236264&utm_medium=copy
15. https://www.cultureamp.com/blog/improving-the-gender-diversity-of-work-teams/
16. https://hbr.org/2013/12/how-diversity-can-drive-innovation
17. https://www.fastcompany.com/3048342/the-business-case-for-women-in-the-c-suite
18. https://www.unwomen.org/en/what-we-do/leadership-and-political-participation/facts-and-figures

Reach out to the Authors:

website: Authornirajabandi.com
Email: contact@authornirajabandi.com

Social media handles:

Instagram: Niraja565
https://www.instagram.com/niraja565/?igshid=2k9
k6auqxfah

Facebook page:

Niraja Bandi:
https://www.facebook.com/niraja.bandi.3

www.ingramcontent.com/pod-product-compliance
Lightning Source LLC
Chambersburg PA
CBHW051102250726
48656CB00001B/431